Law Enforcement and Technology

Andy Bain
Editor

Law Enforcement and Technology

Understanding the Use of Technology for Policing

Editor
Andy Bain
University of Mount Union
Alliance, Ohio, USA

ISBN 978-1-137-57914-0   ISBN 978-1-137-57915-7 (eBook)
DOI 10.1057/978-1-137-57915-7

Library of Congress Control Number: 2016960038

Cover illustration: Modern building window © saulgranda/Getty

Printed on acid-free paper

This Palgrave Pivot imprint is published by Springer Nature
The registered company is Macmillan Publishers Ltd.
The registered company address is: The Campus, 4 Crinan Street, London, N1 9XW, United Kingdom

Acknowledgment

With thanks to our friends and colleagues in law enforcement and criminal justice services around the world; we live in times both strange and challenging, but always rewarding.

CONTENTS

CONTRIBUTORS

Andy Bain Department of Sociology and Criminal Justice, University of Mount Union, Alliance, OH, USA

Louis P. Carsone Department of Public Safety, Hubbard, OH, USA

James A. Conser Department of Sociology and Criminal Justice, University of Mount Union, Alliance, OH, USA
Department of Criminal Justice and Forensic Science, Youngstown State University, Youngstown, OH, USA

Brandon J. Courtney Department of English, Passaic County Community College, Paterson, NJ, USA

William J. Mackey Department of Criminology, Indiana State University, Terre Haute, IN, USA

Bryan K. Robinson Department of Sociology and Criminal Justice, University of Mount Union, Alliance, OH, USA

Andrew Turowski Chief of Police, Louisville Police Department, Louisville, Ohio, USA

LIST OF FIGURES

LIST OF TABLES

CHAPTER 1

An Introduction

Andy Bain

Abstract This first chapter is an introduction to the book. It contextualizes the discussion to follow and sets out the argument for the continued need to develop our individual and service understanding of such an important and fast changing area. The chapter provides a short outline of the historical nature of policing, and their position as local and national agencies of state control, to support the community. In the final section the chapter provides the reader with an outline of the chapters to follow and how this will help to inform their own knowledge and understanding of this important topic.

Keywords Policing futures · Technology · Community policing

The Police (Developing the Service)

It is a little short of 200 years since the first formal police force was introduced to the city of London, and in that (very) short period we have seen law enforcement grow from a single city force into an internationally recognized brand, providing for the same structure, uniformity,

A. Bain (✉)
Department of Sociology and Criminal Justice, University of Mount Union, Alliance, OH, USA
e-mail: bainaj@mountunion.edu

© The Author(s) 2016
A. Bain (ed.), *Law Enforcement and Technology*,
DOI 10.1057/978-1-137-57915-7_1

1

and service to their local and national communities. It is a development which has been premised upon a service to the community which speaks to the best parts of our social being, the wish to provide a safeguard, to support those in need. Indeed, a quick search of almost any police force, local, national, or international, finds a mission statement which (broadly) espouses that same message. The London Metropolitan police mission states that they seek to make *London safe for all the people we serve*. Similarly the Queensland Police Service in Australia states, *With Honor We Serve*, and the prevailing standard that has become instantly recognizable is that of the LAPD motto *To Protect and to Serve*, which has remained in service for 50 years (and more). It is a symbol of our work, and it communicates an intention.

Policing, more generally its role and the services it provides, make for an extremely interesting discussion, and although the concept of policing can be dated as far back as the ancient Egyptians, it is in its more modern form – as a service to enforce the laws of the state, to maintain order, to provide safety, security, and support, to the local community – that it is more easily recognizable today.

That is not to say that historically we lived in a society devoid of structure, organization, or any recognizable form of policing. Indeed, this is a subject of great interest to many authors (see for example Barrett and Harrison 1999; Emsley 1999; Fuhrmann 2012), but prior to Sir Robert Peel's introduction of the Police (reform) Act of July 1829, policing was rather an *ad hoc* system of governance. A system, which, really did depend upon your ability to work for, or pay for the securities that we tend to take for granted today. Even still, it was not as smooth an introduction as it appears in the textbooks. It has required great interest and innovation on the part of certain individuals, in order to keep pace with, and even develop new forms of policing, which has taken place over a (comparatively) very short, but immensely, proud history. Yet it was/is a field replete with opportunity, and through the development of technologies much of the work of the early officers was thrust into the public eye – an area of great interest for the following chapter.

Technology plays an even greater part in our lives today, than perhaps anybody could truly have imagined just 20–30 years ago, yet its involvement and intertwined relationship with policing has remained constant. Indeed, Deflem (2002: 453) has noted that "technological advances are particularly relevant for policing because they are seen to influence the organization and practices of [the] police." Schultz (2008) agrees, and states that technological changes in policing are happening so quickly, that the same technologies in common use today were not even common knowledge just a few years ago. Indeed, the one constant has been the evolution of technology for use in policing. Examples of this can be found in the development and use of photography, the two-way radio, body armor, and DNA analysis, although there are so many more. This text provides just a little clarity, adding some depth to the knowledge and understanding of such a fast moving field.

Although this text is not truly a comparative analysis of policing and use of technologies, being based predominantly in the experiences of the United States, the broader issues raised here are certainly applicable to a much more widely based social discourse. That said, we acknowledge that there are some service, policy, and even demographic differences which exist. For example, there are a number of countries in which officers do not routinely carry firearms: Iceland, Ireland, New Zealand, Norway, and the United Kingdom (with the exception of Northern Ireland), all spring to mind. However, each of these countries also has access to specialized units (the United Kingdom is one such country which makes use of specially trained officers to perform the duty rather than arming all officers), or the limited use of firearms (in Norway, for example, officers may be issued a firearm, which is kept locked inside the vehicle and is not carried on a routine foot patrol). Further to this, it is also important to recognize that we are discussing *the use of technology for policing*. Thus, although the argument can be made that experience differs, it is still the case that each service will make use of similar equipment, tactics, and training, when using patrol vehicles, body armor, cameras, photography, forensics, computer sciences, and so much more.

With these points in mind, although much of our terminology and discursive analysis is based in the policing and law enforcement of the United States, we are quick to acknowledge that just as much innovation and technological advance has taken place in a host of other global settings. Policing is no longer a local affair, and what takes place in England, France, Germany, Italy, Australia (to name but a few countries) today will have a bearing upon North America tomorrow, and this is just as easily reversed. Indeed, the vision and mission statements of the International Association of Chiefs of Police (IACP) states that "IACP serves the leaders of today and develops the leaders of tomorrow," concluding that "IACP is dedicated to advancing the law enforcement profession through advocacy, outreach, education and programs" (IACP 2015: para 1). This then is far removed from the insular and self-serving interests of the first law enforcement departments, and speaks more to the community of policing and society as a whole.

In fact, the period from the 1830s through to 1920 is often seen to be the first period in "modern" policing, the so-called political era – synonymous with the influence of powerful individuals, and the drive and motivations they may have had for the protections of their own social position rather than (perhaps) the altruistic behavior that we associate with policing today. Reppetto (2010) has noted that in England the rise of modern policing may have had more to do with the feared rise of the "criminal masses," than it had to do with the protection of the social whole. This is similarly reflected in the close ties which existed between the local councilmen (politicians) and the elected police officials and officers in the United States (as noted in Chapter 2 of this text). Nevertheless, the fact remains that whatever the purpose of its historical beginnings, modern policing quickly developed into a service for the investigation, and the examination, of criminal behavior, supporting the rights of the individual within the social group. It is a service which we have become familiar with and come to expect today.

THE STRUCTURE OF THE BOOK

There are three themes evident in the book: (1) Technology past and present, (2) Supporting Community Policing, (3) The Application and Reality of Policing and Technology, and we have divided the text accordingly. In the first two chapters we offer a short history of the development of technology as used by law enforcement departments – rather than technology *per se*. In Chapter 2 Andy Bain examines the history and development of technologies, from the early history of modern policing through to the end of the twentieth century, and makes use of a number of examples to provide an indication of just how quickly things have changed, and developed, in just 200 years of policing. The technology of the twenty-first century is brought into focus in Chapter 3 by Bill Mackey and Brandon Courtney. In this chapter Mackey and Courtney make use of the list of technologies and law enforcement provided by the National Institute of Justice, United States, as their basis for the ensuing discourse, in order to frame the work of police departments in the United States today.

Regardless of the technologies available, unless they are put to good use, there is no advantage. Chapters 4 and 5 are to a greater extent concerned with how law enforcement can put its best foot forward in using modern technologies. In an alternative discussion Andy Bain (Chapter 4) and Bryan Robinson (Chapter 5) discuss the power of communication in serving the community. Communication is something that policing agencies have been accused of being particularly poor at (regardless of where in the world policing has been examined). In many instances, policing is accused of bullying tactics and lacking an understanding of, or providing for any real dialogue with, the local communities. Examples are not limited to, but include, the death of Mark Duggan and the subsequent London riots (2011); the disappearance of April Jones (2013); the death of Michael Brown which sparked the Ferguson (Mi) riots (2014); the use of bullying and intimidation tactics by police officers in Victoria, New South Wales (AU); and the New York police officer – Randolph Holder – who was shot and killed in October 2015. Most recently this has been added to by the devastating shootings of two civilians: Alton Sterling (Baton Rouge, LO) and Alva Braziel (Houston, TX), and the fatal shooting of five officers (Lorne Ahrens, Michael Krol, Michael Smith, Brent Thompson, and Patrick Zamarripa) in Dallas (TX), during the summer of 2016. Thus, in Chapter 4, Bain provides for a discussion of fairness, fair use, and community policing and ways in which communication has been used to serve the police and aid community service. In Chapter 5 Robinson examines the use of electronic, and more specifically, social media to support community relations and aid law enforcement departments in understanding better their community image.

In Chapters 6 and 7 we turn our attention to the realities of technology, its use at the crime scene, and the reality of managing the use of technology. In Chapter 6 Jim Conser and Lou Carsone explore the advancement and development of technologies in use at crime scenes and which can aid the investigation and processing of the scene today, providing further discussion of the technologies related to communications, patrol, crime scene analysis, evidence processing, and crime laboratory equipment. For example, we know that electroshock weapons are a less-lethal alternative to using deadly force, but the specialized functions such as video, details of deployment, and voice recording can document the incident from angles other than the traditional vehicle video and even modern body cameras. In contrast, Chief Andrew Turowski of the Louisville Police Department (OH) provides a discussion of the realities of the use of technology in policing today (see Chapter 7). This provides an opportunity to look at the topic from the perspective of a true professional, and helps us to consider how technology and policing can work together, but may also be a hurdle to overcome if we do not develop our own technology at the same pace as other users. Finally, Chapter 8 rounds out the text with a brief discussion of the future: the use of technology by law enforcement officers/officials. This final chapter is, without doubt, an extremely important discussion to have. As was noted at the head of this introduction, the pace of changes that take place in technology today have never been seen before, and inevitably the more we use that technology, the faster it develops and changes. Indeed, Custers (2012) has noted that technology provides law enforcement with new opportunities for investigation and prosecution, to which we would add that in order to maintain our knowledge and understanding, we need to be both forward thinking and innovative in our own use of technology.

References

Barrett, A., & Harrison, C. (1999). *Crime and punishment in England: A sourcebook.* London, UK: UCL Press.

Custers, B. (2012). Technology in policing: Experiences, obstacles and police needs. *Computer Law & Security Review, 28*(1), 62–68.

Deflem, M. (2002). Technology and the internationalization of policing: A comparative-historical perspective. *Justice Quarterly, 19*(3), 453–475.

Emsley, C. (1999). The origins of the modern police. *History Today, 49*(4), 8–14.

Fuhrmann, C. (2012). *Policing the Roman empire: Soldiers, administration, and public order.* Oxford: Oxford University Press.

IACP. (2015). Vision and mission. Available at: http://www.iacp.org/Mission.

Reppetto, T. (2010). *American policing: A history 1845–1945.* New York, NY: Enigma Books.

Schultz, P. D. (2008). The future is here: Technology in police departments. *The Police Chief, LXXV*(6). Available at: http://www.policechiefmagazine.org/magazine/index.cfm?fuseaction=display_arch&article_id=1527&issue_id=62008.

Andy Bain is Assistant Professor of Criminal Justice at the University of Mount Union, Ohio, USA. He holds a PhD in Offender Behavior, a MSc in Criminal Justice, and a Graduate Diploma in Psychology. Andy is the coauthor of *Outlaw Motorcycle Gangs: A Theoretical Perspective* (with Mark Lauchs & Peter Bell), and previously coauthored *Professional Risk Taking with People: A Guide to Decision-Making in Health, Social Care & Criminal Justice* (with David Carson). In addition Andy has published in a number of leading international academic and professional journals. His professional background includes 4 years with the

National Probation Service (England & Wales) and 6 years running a successful criminal justice consultancy group, providing guidance and advice to offender groups, law enforcement agencies, and correctional bodies. This in turn led to the publication of a number of local and national policing and corrections reports. He is an active member of national and international professional bodies, and his research interests include tattoo and culture, gangs and coded language; policing and social groups; social-psychology of offending and risk-taking behavior; and the (psychological) investigation of criminal behavior.

CHAPTER 2

Horses and Horsepower, Fingerprints and Forensics: The Development of Technology and Law Enforcement

Andy Bain

Abstract The significance of technology in the development of the policing role cannot be denied, and nor can it be overstated, for it provides the tools needed to better understand the criminal act, and to better protect the community in the future. This chapter provides an indication of the technologies, and an appraisal of those same technologies. The chapter situates its argument – for the main part – in the innovation of the nineteenth century, which continued throughout much of the twentieth century. The chapter will conclude with the introduction of DNA analysis. This is done in order to provide for some contextualization of the role technology has played in the last 200 years, as well as to set the ground for what is yet to come in the future.

Keywords Modern policing · Technology · Scientific investigation · Forensics

A. Bain (✉)
Department of Sociology and Criminal Justice, University of Mount Union, Alliance, OH, USA
e-mail: bainaj@mountunion.edu

© The Author(s) 2016
A. Bain (ed.), *Law Enforcement and Technology*,
DOI 10.1057/978-1-137-57915-7_2

9

INTRODUCTION

The story of policing and its relationship to/with technology is a convergence of paths, which have developed separately and completely independently of each other, but are intertwined nevertheless. As was noted in the introductory chapter to this text, in some way, shape, and form, the enforcement of law has been present as a form of social control throughout the history of human society. Wherever there is a social group, there is a policing "force" of some description, charged with the maintenance of order. In a similar way, the advancement of society has required that innovative individuals seek more efficient, more successful, and better equipped systems in order to provide the services we have come to enjoy in our everyday lives. Every so often those two systems collide and provide us with tools that help us to better investigate, examine, and understand the world around us – for good and bad. In terms of the enforcement of law, those same techniques and technologies are applied to enable a better understanding of the crime, the victim, the scene, and – to an extent at least – the offender.

This chapter looks to the development of technologies which have guided (modern) policing since its introduction through to modern day, and will stop short of the end of the twentieth century. The reason for this is twofold. First, such great steps in modern technology were taken throughout the early history of policing that it serves well to discuss those in some depth. Second, it seems redundant to discuss – in what would be such a brief manner – the focus of Mackey and Courtney's chapter, when they have provided such an excellent discourse. Added to this, we (and I'm speaking on behalf of the authors of each chapter here) would argue that a timeline is often very helpful in understanding the development of the service and its organization; and although I am sure that there are a hundred sources that will prove a great resource in examining the history of policing (you may wish to examine Beattie 2003; Emsley 2014; Leishman et al. 2000; or Reppetto 2010, 2014), there are few which deal specifically with the development of technologies in the service of law enforcement (although you may wish to take a closer look at Deflem 2002, for an interesting discussion of technology and its usefulness to international policing). I would add, however, that this is not an exhaustive list. I do not plan the destruction of great swaths of woodland to accomplish this task; I offer here an outline of some of the advances that have enabled the law enforcement services we look to today.

WHERE IT ALL BEGINS

The history of policing and its various applications can be traced through much of human existence. Fuhrmann (2012), for instance, has offered a fascinating discussion of policing in the Roman Empire, reflecting upon the use of military personnel in local provinces to police the populous and maintain some form of public order, and to investigate local grievances or criminal behavior. Eibach (2008) has also provided an excellent discussion of the containment of violence, its policing and prosecution if you will, during the Middle Ages in Central Europe. Indeed, much of the discussion offered by Eibach bears a striking resemblance to the historical development of the Americas during the same period, and throughout much of the nineteenth century, as America sought to establish itself and the pioneers pushed their way further west in an effort to establish new colonies, territories, and states.

This should not be of great surprise, as the Americas were colonized by people from Europe, who brought with them their own customs and practices, including systems of justice and punishment. Part of that would have been the introduction of a policing system not completely alien from that of the old English constabularies notable until the end of the eighteenth century, and the local county Shire-Reeve (or Sheriff) who – as an officer of the crown – held the highest position of law enforcement in the local county.

For much of history then, we can say that the Western world (as we know it today) relied upon a system of patriarchy, in which governance was controlled by local town councils and individuals with power and influence (which may have been financially based). This was an interesting time for the investigation of criminal and deviant behavior as to this point violence had been used as a means of control, which meant that once accused the only way to prove your innocence was to defend your honor in combat. However, as society moved toward a more modern age, the technique of violence lost much of its legitimacy, and the practice of providing evidence to the courts (and with it the proof of guilt) was established as a new standard. This is not to say that individual violence disappeared, but as a tool for local authorities it became less common.

Further to this, Briggs et al. (1996), and Hibbert (2003) have identified the use of thief-takers and runners during the eighteenth and early nineteenth century as being integral to the ways in which we police society today. Thief-takers were paid privateers who would be hired to capture and return the criminal. Usually employed by the victim, they were also able to take payment from the justice of the peace when a criminal had escaped. Barrett and Harrison (1999) provide for an interesting account of thief-takers in London, and reflect upon how – to some degree – they played the role of the first detectives, using their skill and knowledge of the local criminal element to investigate the crime. However the rewards were often pitiful, and perhaps not sufficient to risk one's life for, which may have made it an easily corruptible system. Remember, at this time, the only way that the "criminal" could be identified was by the description given by the victim or court officer, and records were often lacking. This could then result in an innocent person finding themselves on the wrong side of the law, receiving punishment for an offence they never committed.

In the United States similar services were popular in the mid-point of the nineteenth century, and can be seen in the use of privateers such as the Pinkerton Detective Agency, who provided a service to private citizens and to local, state, and federal agencies. However, according to the Pinkerton website (2015), the agency would work on a contract basis only, and did not take reward money, the common form of payment for thief-takers and bounty hunters of the time. This was one of Pinkerton's own code of ethical practices and something he strongly believed in, as offering a professional – all be it private – policing service. The Pinkerton Detective Agency developed much of the same services that the public system had done elsewhere. Yet, the agency also brought with it an air of professionalism often missing from the public service. For example, Pinkerton developed a catalogue of offenders which included their names and a brief description of the person, their method of operation (MO), associates and associated addresses used.

However, as happened with many of the privateers in Europe, as the public service continued a drive toward a professionally based service, the Pinkerton Detective Agency found itself in greater conflict and dispute with local labor groups, organizations, and public law enforcement agencies. That, and the continued drive to provide for a uniform public service, meant that privateers really were no longer in such great demand. As an aside, it is interesting to note that in contrast to the fits and starts that private policing went through during the Victorian period, Button (2007) has noted that the industry now employs more people (worldwide) than the public service, and has found itself with increasing powers and authority – certainly in the private sphere, if not public.

The Science of Investigation

As I noted in the introduction to this chapter, it is har
developing service, without looking to some of the ear
processes or tools. Alongside the scientific processes bei..._
enforcement agencies had begun to take notice of the application oı ௶_
equipment available. In 1836 Samuel Colt had patented the repeat revolver
which enabled the owner to shoot multiple rounds of ammunition in quick
succession without the need to reload between each shot. Alexander
Graham Bell was credited with the invention of the telephone in 1876,
which enabled fast and efficient communication between the officer and
the station house (communication is something that will arise throughout
the text, but can be found to a greater extent in Chapter 4 if this is of
particular interest), and with the introduction of the motor-carriage, the
extended work of law enforcement was not exaggerated. An officer now
had the ability to move between one place and the next in relative safety
and where there was a need, they could do so in quick time, being
dispatched to assist communities which had hitherto been sparsely popu-
lated or supported. They had the ability to move multiple officers, and even
transport offenders. By 1899 for example, Akron Police Department in
Ohio, USA, had already started to mechanize, making use of an electrically
charged wagon for the patrol of the city (Clinton 2010), and although
other cities toyed with the idea, they were seen as expensive and unreliable
additions to the service. A further impact may have been the fact that for
much of the United States, policing was still conducted by the Sheriff
rather than a "local" police department, as much of the country still existed
in isolated, or certainly separated communities, with great distances
between them. Thus, outside of the city districts the use of a motorized
vehicle would have been limited, not something of real worth for departments covering such a large expanse, but which certainly required greater
consideration following the First World War.

However, without these advances of rudimentary technologies and
science, much of the investigative process we expect to take place at the
crime scene today would just not have been possible. From around the
mid-point of the nineteenth century much of the technological advances
we take for granted today really propelled policing into a new age.
Examples of the advances made are bountiful, and those noted here are
only a selection of my own personal favorites, and do not constitute the
totality of all the wonders that have come into being in the last 200 years.

For example, in 1832 John Bodle was arrested for the suspected poisoning of his grandfather. The police requested the help of a chemist James Marsh who then examined the body of the victim. Although initial tests found arsenic, it had deteriorated beyond any usefulness by the time of the trial and Bodle was acquitted on the basis of a lack of evidence. Unperturbed, Marsh was driven to prove his system of examination and in 1836 his "Marsh Test" received worldwide critical acclaim (Saferstein 2016). The test was simple, and rather crude by today's standards, but effective nevertheless. Yet the identification of the substance, or materials, was not enough for a positive identification, and it was other endeavors which enabled new steps in the process. The introduction of photography for example, provided for a much needed addition to the examination of the crime scene and the identification of suspects and victims. In fact, once the process had been developed more fully, it also allowed for the systematic photographing of convicted criminals for the purpose of record-keeping which we still do today.

Photography is often forgotten in the history of policing and technology, but as noted a little earlier, prior to the introduction of photographic evidence many of the criminals were identified by the description provided by the victim and/or any witnesses, and any distinguishing marks, and this was often an imprecise practice. Throughout much of history the practice had been to brand repeat offenders with a hot iron, or to tattoo them with a recognizable mark, thus enabling for easier identification (Wroblewski 2004). Further to this, DeMello (2014) has noted that as far back as Ancient Rome slaves were tattooed with the letter "F" for *Fugitivus*, if they tried to escape, and as a practice, marking of slaves and or criminals was not banned until the latter part of the nineteenth century in Europe and America. Yet, it was a system open to interpretation, misinformation and abuse. Photography, by comparison, allowed for a similar permanency, which not only captured the identifying mark (such as tattoos) and facial features, but could also be used to help the victim and witness make a positive identification, and reduce (though not eradicate) the incidence of abuse and corruption.

According to Pepper (2005), this undertaking was first developed by the French police, who, in 1879, employed a young Parisian man to file away the many descriptions and photographs that had been collected from criminal investigations. So frustrated by the lack of a systematic process, the young man, Alphonse Bertillion, put together a system of identification which – in addition to the photograph – included the measurement of body parts, and wrote a paper that described the system and how to act upon the information provided. The anthopometric system, as described by Bertillion, meant that for the first time we were able to catalogue, and recall information about a particular individual from a visual record, as well as the measurements and identifying markers on the person's body (Deflem 2002). Bertillion's system of measurement and photography are still the *basis* of identification used today in the "mug-shots" taken as the suspect is processed and received into custody.

Bertillion later added to this original system with the introduction of a metric scale used for photographing evidence at the crime scene. Pepper (2005) notes that by measuring the evidence Bertillion was able to identify tool marks and/or footprints left at the scene, in the relative comfort of his laboratory, where he was able to construct and reconstruct the crime scene from the information he had collected. However, it was Edmond Locard – a pupil of Bertillion – who is credited with creating the first crime laboratories to examine evidence collected at the crime scene with that of the suspect. In essence, Locard suggested that whenever two materials (persons or objects) come into contact with one another, there will be a material exchange. By examining the evidence left behind, he said, we would be able to place the offender and the scene together, whether at a house, in a vehicle, at a store, or with an object left at that place. Put another way, what Locard was suggesting is that whenever two things come together they leave behind *trace*, evidence that the two things have come together, placing one thing with another, when stories conflict. Locard's argument, quiet simply is that evidence cannot perjure itself, that physical evidence is just that, evidence that the event took place. Additionally, Locard provided a list of evidence which he believed would provide for trace, which included:

- Botanical material
- Glass, paint chippings, soil, metal
- Gunshot residue
- Paper and fibers
- Fingerprints and hair

The importance of this work was also noted by others, and whilst Locard worked on the classification of evidence, others began to example the specifics of unique markers to criminal identification.

One source of transfer, which had raised a great deal of interest was the fingerprint. Barnes (2011) notes that ridges in the skin had been discussed in some detail since the beginning of the seventeenth century, but it was not until the writing of J. C. A. Mayer – a German anatomist – in the mid-part of the eighteenth century that the uniqueness of the skin ridges was fully recognized. In fact, it was a full century after Mayer's work that the application of friction ridge skin (or fingerprints) analysis, to law enforcement, became evident. Sir Henry Faulds is credited with being the first person to recognize, and publish on the value of the use of fingerprints in the investigation of crime, and stated their individual nature as being critical to the identification process, with no two people having the same ridge print, and no two fingers being the same (Barnes 2011). It may seem obvious to us today, but until those first examinations, the presence of evidence left behind by the offender had never truly been considered or understood.

PROFESSIONALIZATION AND POLICING

There was however, much more to the start of the twentieth century, some of which undoubtedly had a bearing upon social movements toward change and which may have raised questions of integrity, rigor, and professionalism in every field. Don't forget, many of the police departments of the latter part of the nineteenth and early twentieth century were seen to be easily controlled, ineffective, and corrupt agencies, in the service of politicians and political parties, rather than the local community, owing to the fact that commercial leaders and politicians were usually the same people that made decisions about who to employ on behalf the town/city, and also those seen to have the greatest investment and interest.

Society, both in Europe and the United States had changed greatly with the advent of the First World War, a so-called total war, in which more than six million people lost their lives. The total devastation of this conflict cannot be counted simply in terms of those that lost their lives in the defense of others, but is also evident in the ways in which people saw their place in society, and what the social group (and more specifically their community) meant to them. Socially, there were calls for reform, driven – at least in part – by the devastating economic downturn which had quickly followed the initial boom of the 1920s, and a belief that society should provide for better and more supportive environment, better equipped to deal with social problems which impacted upon the lives and living conditions of its citizens.

It was a period of social reform which recognized the need for public accountability and ethical practice, and may account for Johnson's (1981) suggested reforms of the police that took place at the same time. There was an expectation of professional standards (throughout society), which brought with it a belief in a community free from criminal activity and a professional public police service set up to be the defense against crime and disorder (Kelling 1988). Thus, Kelling and Moore (1988) are able to argue that just as there may have been an expectation of the development of professionalism in many other quarters, policing was no different.

The professionalism of policing throughout the world required a greater understanding of the process of investigation and the use of many of the tools and services which only 100 years before would not have existed. The transformation from early beginnings to a professional service, is truly remarkable, adding science as well as technology, in the form of such things as the polygraph and DNA analysis. Yet, it is perhaps the introduction of the two-way radio and the development of a reliable and cheaply maintained automobile, which best exemplify the development of policing technologies during this period, as both were instrumental to the everyday work of the officer.

As noted earlier, the introduction of the first mechanized patrols were seen to be expensive and unreliable, and were not supportive of the work of the officer in their daily duties. This is not to say that some departments did not embrace the introduction of mechanized patrol, indeed Detroit (MI), and Evanston (IL) introduced motorcycles to the service in 1908 (Bond 2014), but it was with the introduction of, first the Ford Model T, and the development of the V8-Flathead Model B in 1932, that the popularity of the motorized patrol vehicle expanded. Importantly, Ford had realized that cost and reliability were of great importance to both the public and public offices/institutions and in his new production line vehicles, both of these issues were attended to.

There was of course a secondary reason for the development of a mechanized police, and that was in the fact that criminals readily embraced this new technology. One example is that of prohibition, a lucrative business opportunity if you had the means to manufacture and distribute your goods. Poverty, coupled with mass unemployment, provided for a readily available workforce, and the automobile made the distribution of alcohol fast and effective, which in turn enabled the criminal groups an opportunity to distribute to a much wider client base, and left many smaller, local, police departments at a great disadvantage.

Yet even as the popularity of the automobile and the motorcycle grew, the greatest issue for the policing of such criminal groups had been the ability to communicate and coordinate their efforts. Although the introduction of the one-way radio in Detroit, Michigan in 1928 is of great significance, and made great strides in combating the criminal and organized groups, it is the two-way radio – introduced in Boston just 6 years later – which was to have a more lasting impact upon the way that the police department(s) were able to communicate, coordinate, and control efforts on the streets. There were for example, a number of issues with the one-way radio system. Whilst the one-way radio was able to inform the officer of where they needed to be, or of a crime in progress, there was no way of knowing if anybody was in attendance or even if they had heard the transmission, as transmission was a problem unto itself. These early radio systems worked on commercial airwaves in much the same manner as any other radio stations, and often at low or very low frequency, which meant if there was a large building, railroad lines, or heavy construction taking place, the signal was unreliable and certainly proved disruptive for many of the intercity departments. Nevertheless, the one-way system was a great improvement, on the previous system which relied upon the officer to place a call to the dispatch center to be provided with information regarding an incident which requiring their attention. The alternative was to have officers placed in close proximity to each other enabling them to respond to the hue and cry of an officer requiring support.

In contrast the two-way radio provided for an advancement of a proactive rather than reactive system of policing. This meant that the officer was able to initiate contact with the dispatch center, if they believed there was a need, rather than waiting for the decision to be made on their behalf. Even though it was to become the bedrock of all communication systems for law enforcement around the world, the two-way radio was an expensive investment for any police department. In-car transmitters at that time could cost upwards of $700 making them more expensive than the patrol car itself. In addition, they were still making use of the same radio frequencies as commercial services which meant that listening in on police communication became a popular pastime, but also meant that the criminals they were trying to pursue also had the same ability to hear them coming. Today, this same system still makes up for the best part of the communication between officers and colleagues, and the dispatch center and will continue to do so – although in new and innovative forms – for the foreseeable future (Griffith and Clark 2014).

Cost can be prohibitive, and for many local departments the benefits of such changes are often hard to see, until much later (something that Turowski will address in Chapter 7).

THE SCIENCE OF POLICING

The same argument of weighing the positives against the negatives can be made for a number of other fields of investigation of course, but the benefits of such services can have a great impact upon our ability to do the job. Support for the investigative process provided by the (forensic) laboratory setting has, for example, helped guide and develop much more besides one single technology. As noted above, the creation of the first crime laboratory is credited to Locard, who in 1910 opened a laboratory specifically dedicated to the examination of evidence collected at the crime scene. This first crime laboratory was opened in Lyon, France, and its early successes led to its official recognition by the police department in 1912. This was later followed by the LAPD, who made a conscious decision to open the first crime laboratories in the United States in 1923, and was further supported by the introduction of federal laboratories set up by the FBI in Washington DC, in 1932. Although the setting up and use of this first federal laboratory was well publicized, it seems it was more for public show than it was made use of for the investigative process; services were expensive and took a great deal of time and effort in order to get something of use to the investigation. Nevertheless, this and the addition of a number of polygraph machines propelled the use of (forensic) science into the public limelight and made good use of advances in technology.

By 1948 the American Academy of Forensic Sciences had been formed and held its first national/international meeting, which included advances in the process and examination of fingerprinting, the investigations of the crime scene, and the use of scientific processes for ballistics purposes. Forensic Ballistics, or the identification of firearms and ammunition, had been undertaken previously, but it was the introduction of the comparison microscope in 1927, which enabled the observer to examine two pieces of evidence side-by-side and provided for far greater accuracy in the identification process. Steele (2008) notes that pioneers in firearms identification had suspected that there were grooved patterns which leave individual markings on the ammunition when fired and that each barrel would have its own unique set of imperfections. These markings – although invisible to the naked eye – would enable a ballistics examiner to identify the individual firearm, thus requiring the use of a comparison microscope. Today ballistics experts may also examine trajectory (the path followed), velocity (speed), and distance, as well as the type, make, model, and individual markings of the firearms and ammunition.

Throughout the second half of the twentieth century, many of the strides taken in technologies were advancements in equipment and services already in existence. However, the advent of computerization, the introduction of the National Crime Information Center (in 1967), and computerized dispatch all supported greater change. In addition the introduction of the 911 service (and later the non-emergency service – 311 in the United States, and 101 in the United Kingdom) made great strides in the services provided to the public. This period really can be seen as a movement more toward the service of the community and what would later be recognized as community policing (Stone and Travis 2011). Interestingly however, although considered to be the professional era (the point in time when policing really took on a far greater professional persona), there was little change in the way of police training and despite the suggestions and conclusions of the presidential commission, education standards and requirements remained – for the most part – largely untouched (Bain 2016).

Similarly, this professionalization of policing, meant to increase its ability to do the job of solving crime, and working with communities really and truly remained questionable. There is no doubt that the political and social unrest of the period following the Second World War had a great bearing upon this and the social conflict of the 1960s did little to improve confidence in policing in North America, which are perhaps still bubbling below the surface today. Professionalism, according to Stone and Travis (2011) really meant that the police knew best, and knew what was best for, and how best to police the local communities, providing for a command and control (top-down) structure. Indeed, although providing for technical expertise and management, it was a public relations disaster – represented in the presence of brutality and aggressive tactics to incidents of civil rights and the peace demonstrations.

The decade following the Second World War was seen to be a period of optimism, and affluence, buoyed by near full employment, and with more women employed than ever before, which in turn further supported the development of a consumerist based economy. However, this idyllic image was in deep contrast of the continued social inequality experienced by large numbers of African Americans, resulting in calls for greater recognition and civil rights. The 1960s also saw a number of significant judgments against police practices, which called into question the so-called professionalism of law enforcement, including the Mapp Vs. Ohio (1961) and Maranda Vs. Arizona (1964). Inevitably, demonstrations brought civil rights groups (African American, women, and progressive student groups) into conflict with (predominantly white, male) authorities resulting in previously unseen levels of social/civil dis-obedience (Minkoff 1997). The police could be seen as the enforcers of law and thus positioned to respond to the disorder. Yet, to make use of a civic (community based) service to quell unrest requires the use of force (which runs counter to the stated purpose to *Protect and to Serve* (Los Angeles PD); *Service, Commitment, Community* (San Ramon); or, *Proud to Serve* (Cleveland PD), and so many others), which predictably acts as a catalyst for mistrust and the deterioration of public-policing relationships. This is something that should be considered of great importance for modern day policing and bears some justification where modern day technology (used by both public officials and general populous) capture scenes of excessive force and brutality.

Perhaps the greatest breakthrough in the "fight against crime" can be seen in the scientific advances made in the identification process and the mapping of crime. In this final section of the chapter we will look at the science of genetic identification, but leave the geographic mapping and analysis of crime to Mackey and Courtney (in Chapter 3). The building blocks of human beings have been central to scientific endeavors throughout history, but it was (first) the discovery of and (second) subsequent encoding of DNA (Deoxyribonucleic acids), which provided for some of the greatest and most substantial aids to the investigative process.

Saferstein (2016) reminds us that much of the work in criminal investigations would not have been possible without the work of Landsteiner who first provided for blood types, and the work of Watson and Crick which provided for the subsequent coding of genetic information – DNA. Landsteiner's work made it possible for us to distinguish the blood type (A, B, AB, and O) at a scene, and thus by knowing the blood type of victim and offender it may have been possible to eliminate a number of suspects, where their blood type was not present. Yet, where other evidence was not present, blood type alone could never provide positive identification. That required far greater investigation, which until very recently was not thought possible. In fact the examination of DNA as a means of identification in criminal cases did not take place until the mid-point of the 1980s.

Although its initial discovery can be traced back to the work of the Swiss physiologist Friedrich Miescher, Watson and Crick's discovery of the complexity of the molecules (in 1953) really began to unravel the mysteries of human DNA, and the individual nature of each and every person (Sinden 1994). Watson and Crick noted that DNA is a double-stranded molecule, which (to all intense and purposes) looks like a spiraling ladder, in which each step (on the ladder) contains sugar, connecting a phosphate and a base, and it is the sequencing of the bases which constitutes our genetic code (Pepper 2005). However, DNA examination and analysis remained on the periphery of forensic science throughout much of its history, and would most likely have remained there had it not been for the research and subsequent investigations of Alec Jeffreys and his colleagues at Leicester University, in the United Kingdom.

Jeffreys had been conducting an experiment to trace inherited illness, a study which completely failed in its endeavors, but which revealed a unique stutter in the DNA sequencing. Jeffreys realized that this was a unique marker, as unique to the individual as fingerprints, but at a finite level (McKie 2009). The work of Jeffreys and the team at Leicester University have been put to good use in the short history of DNA examination and profiling, and have seen the work reach far and wide, providing for the exoneration of thousands of innocent people and the capture of thousands of guilty offenders.

Summary

Although this chapter only provides for a very short introduction to some of the key advances, the relationship with policing is undeniable. Today, many of the advances discussed here have been surpassed, perfected, or if not, replaced with bigger, better, and more adaptive technologies – a discussion provided for by Mackey and Courtney (see Chapter 3 in this text). However, what is evident is that without much of the innovation and work of the early investigators (both social and criminal), much of what we take for granted today would never have been possible.

Policing and the investigation of crime, whether public or private, is a system which is all too often examined only for its failings and rarely praised for the innovation and dedication that it takes to provide the services expected by society. According to Custers (2012), police departments all over the world are making use of, and examining, constantly, new and innovative technologies in the fight against crime. Throughout the coming discussions the practice of policing and its use of technology will take us in many differing directions, but perhaps what should be remembered throughout this is that we start from the same principle of good will and a wish to change lives for the betterment of all, and it is often technology that helps us to achieve our principle objective – to serve the community and protect liberty.

REFERENCES

Bain, A. (2016). Education and policing: An expectation of professionalism. *ACJS Today, XLI*(2), 14–18.

Barnes, J. G. (2011). History. In A. McRoberts (Ed.), *The fingerprint sourcebook*. Washington, DC: National Institute of Justice, Office of Justice Programs.

Barrett, A., & Harrison, C. (1999). *Crime and punishment in England: A sourcebook*. London, UK: UCL Press.

Beattie, J. M. (2003). *Policing and punishment in London, 1660–1750: Urban crime and the limits of terror*. Oxford, UK: Oxford University Press.

Bond, M., (2014). Motorcycle police: A tradition of patrol excellence. In *Public service*. Available at: http://inpublicsafety.com/2014/05/motorcycle-police-a-tradition-of-patrol-excellence/.

Briggs, J., Harrison, C., McInnes, A., & Vincent, D. (1996). *Crime and punishment in England: An introductory history*. London, UK: Routledge.

Button, M. (2007). *Security officers and policing: Powers, culture and control in governance of private space*. Aldershot, UK: Ashgate Publishing.

Clinton, P., (2010). History of America's first motorized patrol vehicle. *Police: The Law Enforcement Magazine*. Available at: http://www.policemag.com/blog/vehicles/story/2010/05/story-of-the-first-modern-patrol-car.aspx.

Custers, B. (2012). Technology in policing: Experiences, obstacles and police needs. *Computer Law & Security Review, 28*(1), 62–68.

Deflem, M. (2002). Technology and the internationalization of policing: A comparative-historical perspective. *Justice Quarterly, 19*(3), 453–475.

DeMello, M. (2014). *Inked: Tattoos and body art around the world*. Santa Barbara, CA: ABC-Clio, LLC.

Eibach, J. (2008). The containment of violence in Central European Cities, 1500–1800. In R. McMahon (Ed.), *Crime, law and popular culture in Europe* (pp. 1500–1900). Cullompton, UK: Willan Publishing.

Emsley, C. (2014). *The English police: A political and social history* (2nd ed.). London, UK: Routledge.

Fuhrmann, C. (2012). *Policing the Roman empire: Soldiers, administration, and public order*. Oxford: Oxford University Press.

Griffith, D., & Clark, M., (2014). Radios: Your lifeline is evolving. *Police: The Law Enforcement Magazine.* Available at: http://www.policemag.com/channel/technology/articles/2014/06/radios-your-lifeline-is-evolving.aspx.

Hibbert, C. (2003). *The roots of evil: A social history of crime and punishment.* Stroud, UK: Sutton Publishing Ltd.

Johnson, D. R. (1981). *American law enforcement: A history.* St. Louis, MI: Forum Press.

Kelling, G. L. (1988, June). *Police and communities: The quiet revolution, perspectives on policing.* Washington, DC: National Institute of Justice.

Kelling, G. L., & Moore, M. H. (1988, November). *The evolving strategy of policing, perspectives on policing.* (Vol. 4). Washington, DC: National Institute of Justice.

Leishman, F., Loveday, B., & Savage, S. (2000). *Core issues in policing.* (2nd ed.). Harlow, UK: Pearson Education.

McKie, R., (2009). Eureka moment that led to the discovery of DNA fingerprinting. *Forensic Science – The Observer Newspaper.* Available at: http://www.theguardian.com/science/2009/may/24/dna-fingerprinting-alec-jeffreys.

Minkoff, D. C. (1997). The sequencing of social movements. *American Sociological Review, 62*(5), 779–799.

Pepper, I. K. (2005). *Crime scene investigation: Methods and procedures.* Maidenhead, UK: Open University Press.

Pinkerton. (2015). About US: History, Pinkerton Consulting and Investigations. Available at: http://www.pinkerton.com/history.

Reppetto, T. (2010). *American policing: A history 1845–1945.* New York, NY: Enigma Books.

Reppetto, T. (2014). *American police: A history 1945–2012.* New York, NY: Enigma Books.

Saferstein, R. (2016). *Forensic science: From the crime scene to the crime lab* (3rd ed.). Boston, MA: Pearson Education.

Sinden, R. R. (1994). *DNA structure and function.* San Diego, CA: Academic Press Inc.

Steele, L. (2008). Ballistics. In E. York Drogin (Ed.), *Science for lawyers.* Chicago, IL: American Bar Association.

Stone, C., & Travis, J. (2011, March). *Toward a new professionalism in policing, new perspectives in policing: Executive session on policing and public safety.* Washington, DC: National Institute of Justice.

Wroblewski, C. (2004). *Skin shows: The tattoo bible.* London, UK: Collins & Brown.

Andy Bain is Assistant Professor of Criminal Justice at the University of Mount Union, Ohio, USA. He holds a PhD in Offender Behavior, a MSc in Criminal Justice, and a Graduate Diploma in Psychology. Andy is the coauthor of *Outlaw Motorcycle Gangs: A Theoretical Perspective* (with Mark Lauchs & Peter Bell), and previously coauthored *Professional Risk Taking with People: A Guide to Decision-Making in Health, Social Care & Criminal Justice* (with David Carson). In addition Andy has published in a number of leading international academic and professional journals. His professional background includes 4 years with the National Probation Service (England & Wales) and 6 years running a successful criminal justice consultancy group, providing guidance and advice to offender groups, law enforcement agencies, and correctional bodies. This, in turn led to the publication of a number of local and national policing and corrections reports. He is an active member of national and international professional bodies, and his research interests include tattoo and culture, gangs and coded language; policing and social groups; social-psychology of offending and risk-taking behavior; and the (psychological) investigation of criminal behavior.

CHAPTER 3

Advances in Technology and Policing: 21st Century America

William J. Mackey and Brandon J. Courtney

Abstract The significance of technology in the development of the policing role cannot be denied, nor can it be overstated. Technology has provided the tools needed to better understand the criminal act, and to better protect the community now and in the future. This chapter provides an introduction and appraisal to many of the most common and emerging technologies in policing today. The authors hope that this chapter provides readers a basic foundation for law enforcement's use and adoption of technologies, and how they forge the way in which policing is conducted in modern day America.

Keywords Police · Police technology · Technological advances in policing · Digital policing

INTRODUCTION

In this chapter, we attempt to give a brief overview of the multitudes of existing and developing police technologies. Advances in Patrol, Intelligence, Records & Data keeping, Interrogation, Social Media, and

W.J. Mackey (✉)
Department of Criminology, Indiana State University, Terre Haute, IN, USA
e-mail: william.mackey@indstate.edu

B.J. Courtney
Department of English, Passaic County Community College, Paterson, NJ, USA
e-mail: brandon.james.courtney@gmail.com

A. Bain (ed.), *Law Enforcement and Technology*,
DOI 10.1057/978-1-137-57915-7_3

Advanced Interrogation and Interview Technologies will be discussed. In an ever-changing technological climate, where access to information is principal, what are police agencies doing to stay in alignment?

Specifically, this chapter looks at emerging technologies, such as dash cams, Geographical Informational Systems (GIS), SIMmersion technology in interrogation, License Plate Reader (LPR) technology, Stingray and "Tower Dump" software, biometric technologies and advancements, closed-circuit television (CCTV), and next generation 9-1-1 technologies. This chapter focuses on emerging, present, and future technologies. Consideration is given to technologies that are currently implemented in law enforcement agencies, as well as those that have yet to reach the market, or are still in the developmental phase. Ideally, this chapter will act as a primer for those interested in developing a broader understanding of the use of different technologies in policing, and how they are dispersed amongst agencies and varying populations.

PATROL

In today's ever-changing technological climate, it's imperative that law enforcement agencies stay current on technological advances. With society's shift toward more advanced technologies, law enforcement executives must remain abreast of drastic shifts in technology, as well as maintain what particular technologies can do for their departments and agencies. Through various funding sources, including grants from the National Law Enforcement and Corrections Technology Center (NLECTC), executives must possess the know-how and skills to acquire and adapt advanced technologies in their respective agencies. Not only do advanced technologies act as force multipliers, but police technologies also improve efficiency, effectiveness, and morale. Additionally, police technologies have the potential to increase officer safety in a variety of ways.

Dash Cam

In the late 1990s, an increasing number of lawsuits alleging racial profiling were filed against the state, local, and highway patrol agencies (Westphal 2004). In a concerted effort to thwart biased policing practices, and ultimately return confidence to the public, many departments implemented in-car cameras for routine traffic stops. Creating an unbiased record of events, in-car cameras allowed citizens, as well as departments, to view – and review – encounters called into question. In-car cameras have been extremely beneficial, and by agency reports, far exceed the original goal (Westphal 2004). Currently, 69.5% of all police patrol vehicles are equipped with video systems, and this number will likely continue to increase. The Department of Justice's Office of Community Oriented Policing Services (COPS) provides financial aid to state police and highway patrol; its sole purpose, in fact, is to fund in-car video camera systems (Westphal 2004). In 2000, the first federal awards were dispersed. As shown in Fig. 3.1, county agencies were the first to receive funding, and led Sheriff and special policing agencies by a large margin. By 2003, the COPS Program dispersed $21 million in federal assistance for the purchase of in-car cameras across multiple agencies. As camera technology decreased in price, the routine use of patrol mounted cameras increased exponentially for Sheriff (from 19% to 68%) and special policing agencies (from 1% to nearly *all*) by 2007, where they remain steady today. Additionally, officer safety is a major component of in-car cameras, including self-assessment and critique of actions upon reviewing video from the in-car cameras. Furthermore, many officers report the replaying of videos for report writing. Dash cams enable officers to extract statements for evidence, especially concerning consent searches. In-car cameras also play a major role in court proceedings, where officers are able to recall how probable cause was established.

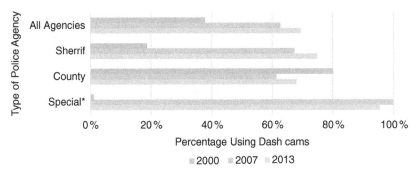

* Special agencies include: Constables office, tribal Police, regional agencies, and primary state agencies.

Fig. 3.1 Police departments using dash cam technology by type of agency for 2000, 2007, and 2013

GIS

Geographical Information System (GIS) allows police departments to store, analyze, interpret, and understand relationships and patterns in crime. In policing, GIS is used in a myriad of capacities. Although GIS does not replace an agency's standard ability to collect and store information in a database, it does enhance law enforcement's ability to use particular datasets (Stoe et al. 2003). GIS works by inputting historical offense, location, and demographic data into a GIS database. The program then outputs a map, which shows areas with higher-than-average crime activity (Stoe et al. 2003). A litany of research shows that places that have a history of high offense rates are, similarly, likely to house the majority of future offenses as well (Eck and Weisburd 1995). This information is invaluable as it allows agencies to provide better distribution of patrol officers in certain areas, focused where crime is much more likely to occur (Eck and Weisburd 1995). Thus, GIS systems help decrease officer response time, increase the chances of apprehension, and increase the likelihood that they will be able to prevent a crime from occurring using the deterrence of officers' presence (Weisburd and Lum 2005). In addition to crime plotting, GIS helps law enforcement agencies further understand why specific crimes might occur in specific areas. For better or worse, GIS has also played a large role in legislation and policing of sex offenders. By locating the residence of sex offenders on a map, agencies are equipped to establish buffer zones between schools, victims, and offenders (Stoe et al. 2003) (Fig. 3.2).

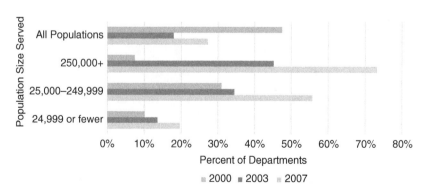

Fig. 3.2   Police departments using crime mapping technologies by size of population for 2000, 2003, and 2007

INTELLIGENCE

Social Media

As technology continues to advance, so too does its social elements. Although social media platforms like Facebook and Twitter are often times benign, police agencies are beginning to implement programs and software that mine users' profiles for intelligence. For example, at the 2013 International Association of Chiefs of Police conference (IACP) in Philadelphia, LexisNexis unveiled its Web-based research service, which electronically "stakes out," potential suspects using cloud based computing and social media sites as part of an agencies' criminal investigations (Gallagher 2013). Although social media is already used by many agencies (with or without specific policy on *how* to use such networks) to combat crime, many large cities, including Boston, have incorporated social media monitoring into their Real Time Crime Centers (RTCC) (Yu 2012). Studies show that the number of agencies using social media, such as Facebook, Twitter, Tumblr, and others, are on the rise, which enables agencies to gather information (Woods et al. 2013). Such information can be invaluable; often, this information is used to locate or interrogate suspects (Woods et al. 2013). Facebook and Twitter are not the only social media platforms targeted, however. Under the Department of Justice's 28 CFR part 23 regulations on criminal intelligence information systems, agencies are tapping into posts and comments made on Tumblr, Google+, YouTube, Instagram, and other "big data" feeds. Using rules-based processing from live source data, it looks for thousands of word combinations within feeds, indicating a range of emergencies and criminal activities (Gallagher 2013).

Social media outlets also act as a way to create increased transparency and communication with the public. According to the Law Enforcement Management Administration Survey (LEMAS) of 2013, nearly 60% of all police agencies in the United States used some form of social media (Twitter, Facebook, Youtube, etc.) to communicate within their communities. Further, it appears that the higher the population served by a police agency, the more likely they are to use social media as a communication tool (discussed further in Bain, Chapter 4; and Robinson, Chapter 5). An analysis of the LEMAS (2013) data shows that 74% of police agencies serving populations over 250,000 residents use *more* than one social media outlet for communication (in contrast to 51% of agencies with populations greater than 25,000 and below 250,000; and only 23% of agencies with populations less than 25,000). This is a logical but important fact, as it shows that police are turning to online platforms in areas where it is difficult to communicate with such a large population.

INTERROGATION

Advanced Interrogation and Interview Technology

For interrogation and interview techniques, strong observation and interpersonal skills are paramount. In the ever-shifting landscape of technology, training a new generation reared on social media and the Internet can present a challenge, however. Traditionally, interrogation techniques were mastered in the classroom, where faculty and peers would learn nonverbal communication cues, as well as varied interviewing techniques (Richmond 2009). Now, companies such as SIMmersion, LLC., have developed software that creates interrogation and interview simulations. The simulation works by having users interact with a suspect named Jennifer Lerner, a creation of the simulator. Through a combination of role-playing scenarios using a prerecorded, live actress, the user is presented with background information on a specific case. One of the advantages of simulators like SIMmersion, LLC., is that it allows the users instantaneous feedback, while demanding the same rigor to nonverbal cues and deception as a classroom. At the close, users receive a score for their performance, which encourages multiple attempts at a confession. The game-like approach to this technology offers multi-use software, one that provides endless scenarios (Richmond 2009). Further, these programs record detailed data while officers work the simulation. Such data are inherently valuable, as it allows for robust quantitative analyses previously unavailable due to the qualitative nature of interrogation (Fu 2014). While the data does not seek to take away from the importance of first-hand interpersonal communication skills and strategies, it does allow for insight into a more evidence-based approach to interrogation (Fu 2014).

RECORDS & DATA

License Plate Tracking

Photographing and tracking thousands of license plates per minute, Automatic License Plate Readers (LPR) are designed to track the movements of drivers (Du et al. 2013; Koper et al. 2013; Grant 2015). Most frequently, these cameras are mounted on police cruisers, road signs, and bridges. Although LPR technology is used to identify individuals who violate traffic signals, other common uses include speeding, automatic toll collection, placing suspects at the scene of a crime, and identifying uninsured motorists. LPR technologies vary in their reliability, too, because of issuing states and countries, font, and complex backgrounds. Additionally, motion blur, light, and noise can affect the quality of the picture (Du et al. 2013). To combat this, LPR cameras require extremely fast shutter speeds and complex software. Using a technology called Optical Character Recognition (OCR), which converts all different types of text (handwritten, digital, differing fonts, etc.) into a digital rendition of the original characters (Du et al. 2013). Recent studies show that License Plate Readers tend to act as a deterrent, and can offer somewhat lasting effects (Koper et al. 2013).

Spying

One of the most controversial technological advances in crime technology is data and intelligence spying. Although the National Security Agency has confessed to siphoning data from citizens, police agencies are increasingly using the same technology to gather data. According to *USA Today* (2013), dozens of agencies around the country are collecting cell phone data from citizens, whether they're under investigation or not. There are many technologies and methods for acquiring cell phone data, many of which use a "tower dump" model of acquisition. This particular method works by giving police information about the identity and location, as well as activity, of any cell phone successfully connected to a cellular tower. The data spans a finite amount of time, however, typically between 1 and 2 hours.

In a single "tower dump," police can acquire data and information from thousands of phones, as well as any wireless provider. Another method of spying is done with the "Stingray." Initially developed for military use, and costing as much as $400,000, this device is aesthetically indistinguishable from a typical cell phone tower (Kelly 2013; Wagner 2013). By tricking all nearby phones within a certain radius to connect to the device instead of a cell phone tower, the Stingray feeds information and data to police. Furthermore, through anti-terror initiatives, the Stingray is mostly funded through federal grants (Kelly 2013). The Harris Co., which manufactures the Stingray, requires its customers to sign a non-disclosure agreement upon purchase (Kelly 2013). Although controversial, police claim these tactics are effective, helping to thwart terrorist attacks, solve crimes, and track abducted children. While police officers need a warrant to search someone's home or vehicle, the same is not required for cellular phone data. As reliance on personal devices, including cell phones, increases, privacy advocates are debating the ethical and legal implications of cell phone spying. Still, cell phone companies store customer data: inbound and outbound calls, location, and text messages.

Biometric Data Collection

Biometrics is the study of human differences, whether those differences appear in a fingerprint's valleys and ridges, the shape and color of the iris, or the structures of the hands. Scientists call these biological differences "chaotic morphogenesis," or random variation in development, whereby each human becomes individualized (Baker 2011). This is the foundation of biometric verification and identification. Verification, although not the most common form of police biometrics, is the most familiar. This type of biometric functions as a cipher, where the user provides biometric data ahead of time. Identification, conversely, is biometric data obtained from a source – a crime scene, for example – and is then compared to an existing biometric database; police agencies, in general, are concerned more with identification, than verification (Baker 2011).

Fingerprints

Fingerprints have been, and remain, the number one biometric tool used by law enforcement agencies. There are several ways to collect fingerprints, but the most familiar form is known as rolling, where ten fingers are rolled on a flat piece of paper. Another, the flat impression, is a sample taken from a single finger. Still another method is called slaps, where four finger samples are taken together. For the majority of the time police have been using fingerprinting, most are kept and stored in physical files, used for reference if a repeat offender is suspected of a new crime and prints are available. Such methods were cumbersome and required very specific information regarding potential suspect print matching. From the increased connectivity of the late 1990s, however, digital fingerprint technologies emerged and became the industry standard. Figure 3.3 shows that the number of departments using digital scanning technology nearly tripled in some cases from 1997 to today,

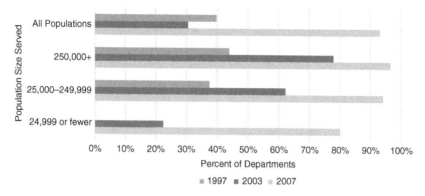

Fig. 3.3 Police departments using digital fingerprinting technologies by size of population 1997, 2003, and 2007

and in 2007 American cities with more than 25,000 citizens have a nearly 100% adoption rate. Originally, prints were taken directly and kept in paper files within the jurisdictional departments.

With the advent of networking, a national database of offenders' prints was created in the late twentieth century, enabling a much faster and more accurate identification system. The Automated Fingerprint Identification System (AFIS) made use of the latest digital imaging to securely store and examine information on many thousands of individuals at a national level. Today, upgraded scanners and new software allow fingerprinting to become much more a science than before, scanned directly into the database with programs that diagram and calculate minutia in individual prints. Although incrementally rolled out, the replacement of AFIS in 2014 with the next generation identification system, termed AFIT, or Advanced Fingerprint Identification Technology, has provided for a much faster, more efficient, system of identification, which has seen an increase from 92% to 99.6% in accuracy (FBI N.D.: para 2), making use of a number of other biometric features.

Facial Recognition

Although fingerprints remain the Gold Standard in biometrics, an increasing focus is being placed on facial recognition (Roufa 2012). As a biometric, facial recognition is not yet as accurate as fingerprinting, although with increasing technological advances, facial recognition software is becoming increasingly more accurate. Facial recognition works by applying different algorithms to measure facial characteristics. Although most of the software is copyrighted, researchers at biometric laboratories continue to advance the technology, applying more and more reliable systems. Interestingly, a current focus in facial biometrics is the ear. It is recognized as a facial feature that tends to change very little over the course of adulthood, allowing increased accuracy in identification (Roufa 2012).

Currently, facial recognition is more widely accepted overseas (specifically in the United Kingdom). Using facial width-to-height ratios and a 128-point facial modeling program, cameras around the United Kingdom attempt to identify possible wanted felons in large public spaces (Gorodnichy et al. 2014). As such, any empirical evidence on the effectiveness of facial recognition comes from UK research. A meta-analysis of 18 studies shows that there is a significant, but small, effect of facial recognition with crime prevention – citing an overall reduction in crime of only 4% (Welsh and Farrington 2002). There was a highly significant reduction in crime when CCTV was used in a UK parking lot controlled experiments, however, where a 41% reduction in vehicle crimes were shown against the control group (Welsh and Farrington 2002). Although not as many studies have been conducted in the US, no significant crime prevention effect has been found for CCTV in North America (Welsh and Farrington 2002).

Iris Recognition

Similarly, as with fingerprints or ear shape, the iris is unique to each individual. Not even identical twins share the same iris. As a method of verification or identification, iris recognition is not as reliable as fingerprinting or facial recognition, because no technology yet exists to get near a subject's iris without his or her consent (Baker 2011). Furthermore, retinal scans and iris scans are not the same in biometrics. Where both forms of biometrics are unique to individuals, the difference is visibility. Retinal veins and nerves are not on the surface of the eye, but instead buried deep within the head. Retinal scans require extreme cooperation from the user, too, which makes identification very difficult. Retinal scans are ideal for access control, however, and the U.S. Department of Defense and the Strategic Air Command of the U.S. Air Force have both used retinal scanning for access control purposes (Baker 2011).

SAFETY AND TECHNOLOGY

Body Cameras

The August 2014 shooting of Michael Brown, and the subsequent protests that were staged in Ferguson, Missouri and around the country, placed the issue of body cameras in the media spotlight (Stanley, ACLU 2015). The choking death of Eric Garner in New York City just a year later, an incident that was captured on video, furthered the discussion and debate surrounding body cameras and the role they will have in the future of policing. Body cameras have several different names: on-officer recording systems, cop cams, and body cams. Body cameras are small, and are worn or clipped onto an officers' uniform, where others are worn as headsets (Stanley, ACLU 2015). The purpose of all body cameras is to record both audio and video of officers' interactions, whether publicly or privately. Although there is still debate about the efficacy of body cameras, research has been done on the perceived benefits, such as: strengthening police accountability, preventing confrontational situations, resolving officer-involved incidents and complaints, improving agency transparency, identifying and correcting internal agency problems, strengthening officer performance, and improving evidence documentation (Stanley 2013; Toliver 2014). Strengthening police accountability works by documenting interactions between the officer and the public, and may even go some way toward addressing concerns regarding interactions between the public and the police (See Bain, Chapter 4).

Even if body cameras deliver on all of their perceived benefits, one must consider implementation and privacy concerns. Not only are privacy concerns paramount, but also community relations and internal departmental affairs. Agencies must also examine the reliance and expectations cameras have on court proceedings, credibility, and financial considerations (Miller and Toliver 2014). Unlike other surveillance equipment like CCTV or License Plate Readers (LPR), body cameras record both audio and video, and capture close-up encounters, opening the possibilities for facial recognition technologies (Miller and Toliver 2014). Whereas stationary cameras and surveillance equipment generally occupy public arenas, body camera technology is utilized inside private residencies and places of business. In addition to privacy concerns, the storage of body cam footage ought to be considered. How long can an agency store private footage? Is there a standard protocol in place if private footage is leaked online? Although points further considered by Turowski (in Chapter 7), these, and other considerations, must be acknowledged, and a balance must be struck between transparency and the governing agencies. Police agencies must also decide when to record. There are two considerations here: police ought to record all encounters in public, a practice, which the American Civil Liberties Union (ACLU) promotes (2014). This includes, but is not limited to, citizens asking for directions, routine traffic stops, and informal communications. The other is a selection-based practice, one where the officer decides when and where to activate his or her camera. The Police Executive Research Forum (PERF) believes the operation of the camera ought to be at the discretion of the officer (Miller and Toliver 2014).

Assessing the effectiveness of body cams has seen a recent boom in the academic literature. In a recent randomized controlled experiment, researchers studied the effect of body camera use by police on use of force and filed complaints by citizens (Ariel et al. 2015). Ariel et al. (2015) found that after 12 months, officers that wore body cameras were only half as likely to use force as those without. Further, the number of complaints filed against officers wearing cameras were reduced from 0.7 complaints per 1,000 contacts to 0.07 per 1,000 contacts, a significant decrease even at such low original rates (Ariel et al. 2015). Citing five additional studies, White (2014) compiled their findings to conclude that, in fact, body cams do significantly impact behaviors: they decreased the number of use of force incidents, improved citizen behavior when interacting with police, expedited any lawsuits or complaints filed, increased conviction rates with arrests, and helped guide training for new recruits. Consistent concerns were noted to include privacy constraints and resource management, including data storage and retrieval (White 2014). According to the most recent LEMAS survey in 2013, currently in the United States, 35% of all agencies are using body cams, if only on a select few officers per agency.

Less-Lethal Force

In the line of duty, police officers will sometimes face violence and noncompliance. The use-of-force protocol is in place for these very scenarios. With advancing technologies, however, less-lethal force provides an alternative for officers put in harm's way (NIJ 2011). The primary aim of less-lethal force is to minimize the possibility of injury or death if an officer is threatened with violence. The decision to use less-lethal force, as opposed to deadly force, is in large part determined by each officer's governing agency. Most agencies have established practices (the "Use of Force Continuum") that help guide the officer as to the appropriate amount of force necessary to gain compliance. Training programs are also in place, which provides officers additional resources for deciding whether or not to use less-lethal force, and in which circumstances. The most popular current less-lethal force to develop out of emerging technology is the Conducted Electrical Weapon.

Conducted Electrical Weapons (CEW) are known by a litany of different names: Tasers (which is an acronym, standing for Thomas A. Swift's Electronic Rifle), conducted energy devices, electroshock weapons, and electronic control devices are some of the most prevalent. CEWs are a less-lethal weapon designed to provide an alternative to lethal force, bringing a potentially violent scenario to a safe conclusion. Initially, the Taser brand CEW implemented gunpowder to fire the electrified darts; subsequently, it was classified as a firearm. Because of its classification, the Taser was not widely distributed (Roufa 2012).

The newer class of CEWs, however, works by firing two metal probes connected to a charged cartridge of compressed gas. Through thin copper wires, the darts remain connected to the target, and up to 50,000 volts of electricity is carried to the target (Roufa 2012). The probes, or darts, enter the target's skin, but the probes can be just as effective if embedded in clothing, as long as the probes make contact with, or remain close to, the skin. For the most effective incapacitation, the probes ought to be spread as far apart as possible. The Taser incapacitates its target through Electro Muscular Incapacitation (EMI): an electric pulse is passed between probes, disrupting neuron communication between the targets' muscles and brain, which in turn causes muscles to tense (Kunz et al. 2012; Roufa 2012). The target cannot engage muscle groups for the charge cycle's duration, usually around 5 seconds.

In the early 2000s, there were still major concerns about the safety of CEWs on humans. Much of the population thought that receiving such a shock could easily cause heart complications or permanent muscle conditions. Research, however, shows that while there is still the small possibility for indirect harm, ECWs are an overall medically safe and effective tool for police to use for compliance (Kunz et al. 2012). Looking at data from the last decade of LEMAS surveys, we can see that use of ECWs by all police agencies has increased exponentially in recent years. In 2003, only 24% of police agencies used ECWs as a less-than-lethal option, increasing to 61% in 2007, and peaking at 76% in 2013 (see Fig. 3.4). Municipal and County

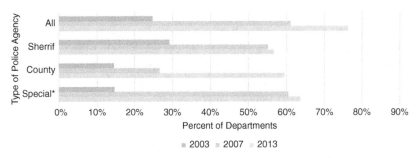

Special agencies include: Constables office, tribal Police, regional agencies, and primary state agencies.

Fig. 3.4 Police departments authorizing the use of conducting energy weapons by type of agency for 2003, 2007, and 2013

agencies saw the most significant rise in ECW use, moving from only 14% in 2003 to 59% in 2013.

Given the aforementioned large increases in adoption, it is paramount that ECWs are also a safe less-than-lethal option. NIJ (2008) research supports the use of ECWs and finds there is no conclusive medical evidence that indicates a high risk of injury or death. Of course, this does not mean ECWs are completely risk-free: barbs and darts can leave puncture wounds and burns; head injuries from muscle incapacitation and falling can occur. Indirect affects have also been shown to result in injury or death if CEWs are deployed against a suspect in water (resulting in drowning), steep incline, or around flammable materials. If proper protocol and deployment is used, however, these risks fall to a minimal level (NIJ 2008). This makes mandatory training and continuing education a necessity for police in order to keep risks of using ECWs at a minimum.

ELECTRONIC SURVEILLANCE

CCTV

Closed-circuit Television (CCTV) is a camera technology that monitors public spaces. Like many technologies discussed in this chapter, the public is wary of privacy issues associated with CCTV and constant surveillance. Still, the Federal Government and the National Institute of Justice have funded research for CCTV, primarily for its use in policing applications "in both the domestic and international arenas" (NIJ 2003). Although CCTV is not a new technology – Great Britain has implemented CCTV for many years as a general crime deterrent and (more recently) terrorism deterrence. As mentioned previously, widespread use of close-circuit television technology is not as popular in America, although its use does appear to be increasing.

Given the controversy of the privacy and effectiveness surrounding CCTV, one arena that remains unaffected is corrections. For years, closed-circuit television has been used in facilities to decrease the number of officers needed to monitor inmates, allowing law enforcement personnel to keep an eye on a large number of housed and incarcerated inmates. Close-circuit television is also used as a cost-saving mechanism in court hearings and procedures (NIJ 2003), allowing inmates to appear in court without having to pay for their travel or associated costs. As with any technology, CCTV has its downsides, which are two-fold: the technology itself (glitches, resolution, storage, cost … etc.), as well as its need for physical placement of monitors and cameras. Exposed cameras can be vandalized, leading to increased maintenance costs and inefficient documentation of a crime. Positioning cameras can also reduce the camera's effectiveness. For example, complex geographies, like some cityscapes, present a challenge for camera placement and monitoring.

Although CCTV has direct surveillance effects, it can also have both unintentional positive and negative effects. For example, a phenomenon commonly referred to as a "diffusion effect," or the idea that security and law enforcement personnel can more effectively monitor areas outside of the camera's reach, thus lowering crime rates even outside of the immediately surveilled areas (Clarke 1997; Weisburd et al. 2006). On the contrary, there can also be a "displacement effect," which pushes crime outside of the surveilled areas to other localities where CCTV is not implemented (Clarke 1997; Weisburd et al. 2006). Indirectly, cameras might offer citizens a false sense of security, leading to a more relaxed view of his or her surroundings (Welsh and Farrington 2015).

Next Generation 9-1-1

With society's ever changing technology, many antiquated law enforcement systems are receiving upgrades. Next Generation 9-1-1 (NG9-1-1) is one such system, utilizing text messaging, video, photographs, and images to upgrade its outdated telephone technology (Dodge and Flaherty 2014). One problem 9-1-1 call centers are facing is how to transfer calls from one center to another. If, for example, call volume exceeds the available resources for a particular center, there is no way to transfer such calls to another center and, subsequently, no way to alert the proper Emergency Management Technicians or police officers. NG-9-1-1 is an Internet Protocol (IP) system that allows digital information to freely flow through the 9-1-1 networks (9-1-1.gov n.d.). Led by the U.S. Department of Transportation (DOT), recent technological advances will allow 9-1-1 to better serve communities and citizens that rely on voice-over-Internet-protocol telephony technologies (voIP) like Skype or Vonage (Dodge and Flaherty 2014). Allowing for an IP-based 9-1-1 system, call centers are more easily able to interface with a wide range of technologies, including cellular devices and computers. The new system will also be able to more accurately and quickly track the location of the caller, while automatically identifying the communication technology being used by the caller, which will then be forwarded to the appropriate first-responders.

SUMMARY

The overarching goal of policing is, invariably, to "protect and serve." As noted throughout this chapter, changing technologies have not only increased efficiency, but have also helped to make communities safer, conduct more thorough investigations, and helped create a safer means of offender detection and apprehension. Technologies such as dash cams, body cams, CCTV, electronic control weapons, networked databases, and upgraded emergency services have ushered in a new era of policing abilities and capabilities. We must be careful, however, that technologies do not get ahead of our defined laws and basic rights (a discussion picked by Turowski in Chapter 7). More technologies and increased networking allows for the collection of large amounts of personal data. Thus, it is important to ensure that checks and balances are intact before wide adoption of any new technologies. Regardless, we can be certain that as new technologies develop and networking grows, we will see them integrated into police agencies and the work of patrol officers. It may be that the future of policing requires as many or more IT personnel on the force as actual officers on the streets.

REFERENCES

9-1-1.gov. (n.d.). *Next generation 911 (NG911)*. Available at: http://www.911. gov/911-issues/standards.html.

Ariel, B., Farrar, W. A., & Sutherland, A. (2015). The effect of police body-worn cameras on use of force and citizens' complaints against the police: A randomized controlled trial. *Journal of Quantitative Criminology, 31*(3), 509–535.

Baker, T. J. (2011, April). *The police chief.* Retrieved September 21, 2015, from Biometrics for Intelligence-Led Policing: The Coming Trends. http://www.policechiefmagazine.org/magazine/index.cfm?fuseaction=display_arch&arti cle_id=2358&issue_id=42011#.

Clarke, R. G. Ed. (1997). *Situational crime prevention.* Monsey, NY: Criminal Justice Press, pp. 53–70.

Dodge, L. D., & Flaherty, L. (2014, June 24). *Intelligent transportation systems joint program office.* United States Department of Transportation. Available at: http://www.its.dot.gov/ng911/.

Du, S., Ibrahim, M., Shehata, M., & Badawy, W. (2013). Automatic license plate recognition (ALPR): A state-of-the-art review. *Circuits and Systems for Video Technology, IEEE Transactions on, 23*(2), 311–325.

Eck, J. E., & Weisburd, D. (1995). Crime places in crime theory. *Crime Prevention Studies,* pp. 1–33. Available at: http://citeseerx.ist.psu.edu/view doc/download?doi=10.1.1.362.1293&rep=rep1&type=pdf.

FBI (N.D.). Next generation identification. Federal Bureau of Investigation – Services. Available at: https://www.fbi.gov/services/cjis/fingerprints-and-other-biometrics/ngi.

Fu, Q. (2014). *Validation of interpersonal stances.* Netherlands: Ensched.

Gallagher, S. (2013, November 13). *Staking out Twitter and Facebook, new service lets police poke perps.* ArsTechnica. Available at: http://arstechnica.com/infor mation-technology/2013/11/staking-out-twitter-and-facebook-new-service-lets-police-poke-perps/.

Gorodnichy, D., Granger, E., & Radtke, P. (2014). *Survey of commercial technologies for face recognition in Video.* Available at: http://cradpdf.drdc-rddc.gc.ca/PDFS/unc198/p800510_A1b.pdf.

Grant, J. (2015). *Automatic license plate recognition.* Department of Computer Science and Engineering. Available at: http://www.cse.nd.edu/~jgrant3/cw/alpr.pdf.

Kelly, J. (2013, August 12). Cellphone data spying: It's not just the NSA. *USA Today.* Available at: http://www.usatoday.com/story/news/nation/2013/12/08/cellphone-data-spying-nsa-police/3902809/.

Koper, C., Taylor, B., & Woods, D. J. (2013). A randomized test of initial and residual deterrence from directed patrols and use of license plate readers at crime hot spots. *Journal of Experimental Criminology, 9*(2), 213–244.

Kunz, S. N., Grove, N., & Fischer, F. (2012). Acute pathophysiological influences of conducted electrical weapons in humans: A review of current literature. *Forensic Science International, 221*(1), 1–4.

Miller, L., Toliver, J., & PERF. (2014). Implementing a Body-Worn Camera Program: Recommendations and Lessons Learned. Washington, DC. Available at: http://www.justice.gov/iso/opa/resources/472014912134715246869.pdf.

National Institute of Justice. (2003). CCTV: Constant Cameras Track Violators. *NIJ Journal* (249), 16.

National Institute of Justice. (2008). *Study of Deaths Following Electro Muscular Disruption: Interim Report.* Retrieved from https://www.ncjrs.gov/pdffiles1/nij/222981.pdf.

National Institute of Justice. (2011, June). Less lethal technology. Office of Justice Programs. Available at: http://www.nij.gov/topics/technology/less-lethal/pages/welcome.aspx.

Richmond, S. (2009, July). Advanced technology for interview & interrogation, *Law and Order*, Hendon Media Group: Law Enforcement Publications and Conferences. Available at: http://www.hendonpub.com/resources/article_archive/results/details?id=2171.

Roufa, T. (2012). *All about TASERS and electronic control devices.* About Careers. Available at: http://criminologycareers.about.com/od/Career_Trends/a/Electronic-Control-Devices-Shocking-Developments-In-Police-Technology.htm.

Stanley, J. (2013). *Police body-mounted cameras: With right policies in place, a win for all.* New York, NY: ACLU.

Stanley, J. (2015, March). *Police body-mounted cameras: With right policies in place, a win for all.* [Electronic] Available at: https://www.aclu.org/police-body-mounted-cameras-right-policies-place-win-all.

Stoe, D., Watkins, C. R., Kerr, J., Rost, L., & Theodosia, C. (2003, February). *Using geographic information systems to map crime victim services.* Office for Victims of Crime, Department of Justice and Crime. Available at: https://www.ncjrs.gov/ovc_archives/reports/geoinfosys2003/welcome.html.

Toliver, L. M. (2014, October). Implementing a body-worn camera program: Recommendations and lessons learned: *COPS*, Vol. 7 (10). Available at: http://cops.usdoj.gov/html/dispatch/10-2014/body_worn_camera_program.asp.

Wagner, S. (2013). Stopping police in their tracks: protecting cellular location information privacy in the twenty-first century. *Duke L. & Tech. Rev., 12,* 200.

Weisburd, D., & Lum, C. (2005). The diffusion of computerized crime mapping in policing: Linking research and practice. *Police Practice and Research, 6*(5), 419–434.

Weisburd, D., Wyckoff, L. A., Ready, J., Eck, J. E., Hinkle, J. C., & Gajewski, F. (2006). Does crime just move around the corner? A controlled study of spatial displacement and diffusion of crime control benefits. *Criminology, 44*(3), 549–592.

Welsh, B. C., & Farrington, D. P. (2002). Crime prevention effects of closed-circuit television: A systematic review. *Annual Review of Law and Social Science, 11,* 111–130.

Welsh, B. C., & Farrington, D. P. (2015. Home Office Research Study 252). *Effectiveness and social costs of public area surveillance for crime prevention.* London, UK: The Research Development, and Statistics Directorate.

Westphal, L. J. (2004, November 9). The in-car camera: Value and impact. *Police Chief Magazine*. Vol. 71 (April). Available at: http://www.policeone.com/: http://www.policeone.com/police-products/police-technology/articles/93475-The-in-car-camera-Value-and-impact.
White, M. D. (2014). *Police officer body-worn cameras: Assessing the evidence*. Washington, DC: Office of Community Oriented Policing Services.
Woods, D., Mackey, W., Rumler, M., Davis, J., & Litchford, H. (2013). On your page, in your head: Police use of social networking information. *Law Enforcement Executive Forum*, *13*(2), 120–129.
Yu, R. (2012, March 18). Social media role in police cases growing, *USA Today*. Available at: www.usatoday.com/tech/new/story/2012-03-18/.

William J. Mackey is an Assistant Professor in the Department of Criminology and Criminal Justice at Indiana State University. His research interests include: Cybercriminology, Social Engineering, Technological Advances in Corrections and Crime Prevention, White-Collar Crime, and Criminological Theory. Bill's current research is focused on correlates of human behavior in data breaches and the application of criminological theory to cybercrime and breach prevention. Bill has published work in the areas of social engineering, advanced crime prevention technologies, and individual differences in both white-collar offenders and hackers. Mr. Mackey is a member of the Cincinnati Bell Digital Forensics Working Group, the National White-Collar Crime Research Consortium, Infragard Partnership for Protection, and the American Society of Criminology. He received a dual bachelor's degree in Psychology and Criminology from Iowa State University, a Master's degree in Criminology from Indiana State University, and is in the process of completing requirements for his PhD in Criminology at the University of Cincinnati.

Brandon J. Courtney teaches as a Developmental English Tutor at Passaic County Community College in Paterson, New Jersey, and is an Adjunct Instructor at Hollins University's Tinker Mountain Writers' Workshop Online. An accomplished poet, Brandon has two full-length collections, *The Grief Muscles* (Sheep Meadow Press) and *Rooms for Rent in the Burning City* (Spark Wheel Press). Additionally, he has a chapbook and full-length collection forthcoming from YesYes Books in 2016 and 2017, respectively. Brandon is a veteran of the U. S. Navy, and received his BA from Drake University in English Writing. He also received his MFA in Creative Writing from Hollins University in 2012, and attended the University of Chicago's MLA program.

CHAPTER 4

Positive Policing: Communication and the Public

Andy Bain

Abstract Communication is perhaps one of the most important aspects of law enforcement, yet it is also perhaps one which is neglected more often than others as being secondary to the important role of the police as crime fighters and law enforcers. However, communication is something that is ignored at an individual's (officer) or agency's peril. This chapter discusses the important role of communication between officers, departments, agencies, and most definitely the importance of good communication with the general public. It will also address some suggestions for how this can be tackled and successfully achieved, thereby providing for a more positive image of the police and in this manner creating a culture of support in the community.

Keywords Community · Communication · Local policing

INTRODUCTION

In a statement to the law enforcement community Estey (2005) made use of the president's message to state the importance of efforts aimed at the improvement of communication in policing, arguing that such efforts are

A. Bain (✉)
Department of Sociology and Criminal Justice, University of Mount Union, Alliance, OH, USA
e-mail: bainaj@mountunion.edu

© The Author(s) 2016   47
A. Bain (ed.), *Law Enforcement and Technology*,
DOI 10.1057/978-1-137-57915-7_4

crucial to the future of the law enforcement profession. However, he was careful to point out that communication is no longer a concern of the use of modern technologies and complex communication systems alone, but also the day-to-day conversations that officers have with members of the local community. In this way we can say that there are two sides to the discussion of communication, and each has two distinct, but related, parts. The first is communication with members of the general public – as community; and second is the communication which takes place within the law enforcement community – between officers, local departments, and state/national agencies.

As such this chapter will – to some extent – provide a similar division of technology and personal communication skills, as a tool of/for communication. It will outline the important role that good communication has in policing local communities today, beginning with a brief discussion of new technologies and the use of electronic media in communicating with the public. Second, it will examine the public image of policing as a base for understanding some of the issues that may arise in communication with the public. I will also highlight some of the main benefits of good communication skills to the individual officer as well as the department (as well as the consequences of poor communication). Finally, I will return to the discussion of electronic media and its use in communicating with the public, which will provide for a useful segway to Robinson's discussion of the public attitudes to policing and the use of social media, in Chapter 5 of this text.

Technology as Communication

As you may have already realized (supposing that you have read the previous chapters in this text), technology has a long and very well established history with(in) policing, and its use in aiding communication is no less evident today than it ever has been. Effective communication is without doubt key to the success of policing strategies, and there is no room for mixed messages or misunderstanding, so the knowledge and understanding of each officer is paramount to their ability to conduct their duties in a safe, effective, and efficient manner.

Even as far back as the end of the nineteenth century, technology was making it possible for officers to keep in contact with each other on the city streets, as well as having constant contact with the local police department or sub-station. Prior to the introduction of the first radios, a series of lights or sirens at particular points on the beat (very often the crossroads of two major roads), were used to draw the attention of the officer, and to indicate that they should contact the department or dispatch officer – and as Turowski notes (see Chapter 7), it was a practice which remained in place for many smaller agencies right through the mid-point of the twentieth century. To this Kelling and Moore (1988) note that by the end of the nineteenth century most cities had introduced a series of call boxes which could be used to maintain order, manage officers on the beat, and inform them when they were needed at a crime scene.

By the mid-point of the 1930s many state agencies and local departments had begun to make use of the two-way radio which greatly improved the communication services between individual officers and the police departments. However, it was not uncommon for local, state, and federal agencies in the same jurisdiction to have multiple communications centers, or hubs, and to work in complete isolation from one another. In fact throughout this period, as a number of agencies fought to establish themselves (see for example the history of the FBI), it was not uncommon for neighboring jurisdictions (or emergency services in the same area) to have compatible services but to choose not to include each other in an information-sharing exercise for fear of losing control of a case or jurisdiction. The benefits of shared communications were not acknowledged until the latter point of the 1980s, and may actually have been as a result of pressures placed on services to find ways in which to save on already stretched budgets and resources.

This seems somewhat alien today, where officers can make use of wireless internet services to check the status of a suspect, or to help relay information between departments or jurisdictions. As Mackey and Courtney noted in Chapter 3, today they can use this same service to run license plates, and check individual identification in a matter of seconds. This can save a great deal of time and energy where previously they may have had to rely on their own knowledge of the individual, or to call it through to the dispatch, duty sergeant, or desk officer.

Technology also brings with it a whole host of exciting opportunities which were previously unknown. Doyle (2014) has noted, for example, that the cell phone can fill gaps which may appear in the use of the (somewhat dated) two-way radio. The issue of cell phones by police departments seems evident and logical. These duty phones no longer serve only as a means to make calls to community groups, or crime victims, but as Doyle (2014) indicates they can act to support the wider duties of the officer. It (the cell phone) also provides for a PDA (personal digital assistant), with a calendar, a notepad, and voice recorder – which can be used for short interviews or personal statements/notes, as well as a digital camera or video recorder, with the capability of relaying digital information instantaneously, and at the touch of a single button.

The relative cheapness of such an electronic device also makes it an effective tool for day-to-day use. Yet, the question does arise as to whether the use of technologies are also another tool acting to isolate the officer from people in much the same way as the patrol car did in the 1950s and 1960s when a drive (no pun intended) for efficiency and effectiveness removed the officer from the streets in favor of speeding up the response-to-call times (an argument made by Kelling and Moore 1988). This certainly would seem to be the case where they would previously have made the effort to visit the individual in person, and which today may result in poorer communications with the community. It seems logical then that there remains a required element of personal contact for the general public to feel that officers are supporting them, and safeguarding their homes (or place of employ) to the best of their abilities.

Conversations with the Public as Communication

One of the most common complaints made regarding policing is the rude and often arrogant attitudes of the officers when engaged with members of the public. This was similarly noted by Barker et al. (2008: 1), who also stated that "when officers adopt such a stance they run the risk of sending a message opposite to the one intended," but which is often the one which sticks in the mind more readily. This may in part be due to the representations we are provided in everyday life, and go some way in explaining the reactions of members of the public when feeling threatened by the approach of an officer or officers. Alternatively it may also go some way in explaining the reactions of officers approaching a scene. As Tooley et al. (2009: 62) state, "Over the course of a career, law enforcement officers see the best and the worst in humanity. They may be thanked for what they do and then spit upon not an hour later." This does not excuse an officer's behavior, but when both the officer and members of the public perceive the outcome of possible interaction as being negative rather than positive, then it is perhaps somewhat easier to see how a public disturbance can arise.

Further to this, Bain et al. (2014) note that invariably people only ever come to understand policing in one of two ways: (1) experience, or (2) consumption. To provide a little more clarity, in the first it is suggested that it is their personal involvement with crime which informs their knowledge of law enforcement (as an offender, victim, or witness), and in the second it is through the consumption of knowledge that we understand the role of law enforcement, i.e. the experience of a friend or family member, or through the images provided by the media (TV film, radio, or print newsmedia).

To this Greer and Reiner (2012) add that the influence of the mass media on our understanding of behavior and the ways in which we represent that behavior will also have an effect upon how we react to that or similar behavior in the future. Therefore, it is possible to argue that when we think of policing today, we are faced with two indelible images: those of the officer of the law-preserving life: the good cop – Chief Inspector Morse (*Morse*[1]), Lieutenant Horatio Caine (*CSI Miami*[2]), Sheriff Walt Longmire (*Longmire*[3]), or Jim Gordon (*Gotham*[4]); the other providing for the preservation of law and order at all costs – Harry Callahan (*Dirty Harry*[5]), or John Luther (*Luther*[6]), or Raylan Givens (*Justified*[7]). For some reason it seems these two images/ideals are dipolar, constantly pushing away from one another and seemingly incompatible with the other. I realize that I have divided these fictional characters into clearly defined groups, and I also realize that in all actuality there are episodes when they show the other side of their character. The important point here is to realize that in any case, there is a justifiable reason for any action they take, and we (the viewers) are forced to conclude that given the same circumstance we would act similarly, because we are able to empathize. We believe that given their situation we would act in a similar way to save the life of our loved one.

In each incidence witnessed (at least in TV and the movies) we are left with a feeling that all was done, only because there was a real danger and they acted in the best interests, and this may be just so. However, the reality is that in the "real" world, we don't always have the benefit of seeing the whole picture, or knowing in advance who the crooks and criminals are, and we may never know why a particular action is needed or necessary, in order to preserve life, liberty, and law and order. For this reason it is important to reiterate that there are many factors which may influence behavior, including our own personal understanding of the world, which inevitably may also act as something which clouds judgment, and understanding of the situation.

This provides for a very delicate set of circumstance for policing. Public image, knowledge, and understanding of local, state, and/or national law enforcement agencies is key to the success of the agency. Without the support of the local community it is unlikely that the (policing) service will be able to provide the level of (public) service required to execute the duties assigned. It is acknowledged that much of the policing takes place in socially disadvantaged neighborhoods (Schneider 1999), owing to the fact that those same neighborhoods will (invariably) also experience the greatest incidents of crime and deviance. However, in terms of policing such neighborhoods, Schneider notes that it is most often the issue of poor communication between the police and the local community which causes the greatest struggle in areas in need of the greatest support.

This was further supported by Herbst and Walker (2001), who stated that although minimal incidents were noted in their own study, language barriers can have an impact upon the delivery of services by local departments, which may exacerbate already strained relationships. Indeed, the use of language codes is something that was first considered in Bernstein's work during the 1960s and 1970s when he found a profound difference in the meanings and use of language. This he said was due to the fact that there was a disconnect in the use of language and its communication, which in turn provide access to, or restricted people from particular situations and circumstance – including opportunities in education and employment. A restricted code produced short grammatically simple sentence structures, using limited vocabulary and is often the experience of individuals from an economically poorer, working class, social upbringing. Conversely the elaborate code is grammatically accurate, logical and descriptive, making use of a much wider vocabulary and provides for a much more detailed account, information, or command. This code is often associated with those of a middle class background and upbringing and who will – inevitably – experience childhood and early adulthood in very different ways.

This is a very simplistic account of what is a truly magnificent piece of social research and I urge you to read Bernstein's work (1961, 1971, 1990) in the original. Nevertheless, for the purposes of our discussion it is possible to say that the disparity in the use of language can be seen in the life experience, life style, and social environments of each individual. Thus those individuals raised in inner city, working class, and poorer environments, often experienced a restricted code and therefore are less likely to understand the complicated and elaborate commands.

One of the examples used is that of the differing language codes used in education. Using Bernstein's suggested elaborate and restricted codes, it is possible to see how this disconnect may occur. For example, the teacher (an authority figure), is a person who by virtue of their position has already completed a higher education, and achieved a middle class status position, and thus perpetuates a middle class language code. The use of complicated and elaborate commands may produce a situation and/or circumstance in which the student becomes frustrated and less cooperative, owing to a lack of experience with such language. In turn this (frustration) becomes the experience of education and teaching, and their position of authority.

To some degree it may be possible to project this on to the wider community and a similar disconnect between the residents of local neighborhoods and the actions taken by the law enforcement officer. For example, the officer is there to work with the community and whilst their role is perceived as legitimate, there is harmony, but once the role is changed to require an unpopular duty (the arrest of a youth) then a sense of social friction can arise. If the arrest involves more than one officer it may be perceived that there is an unjust action and thus the local community may feel disenfranchised or subjugated, and this is when communication is key to a successful resolution.

To counter feelings of community isolation and similar situations, Craven (2009) has suggested the use of further alternate forms of patrol (horseback, bicycle, foot-patrol). This may seem costly, inefficient, and old-fashioned, to some, but where officers have left the comfort of their patrol cars, and taken to the streets on foot, it has also bolstered community partnerships, and increased satisfaction in the role of the officer in the community (Police Staff 2005; Glennon 2010; Bain et al. 2014).

The Skill of Good Communication

Good communication is an art form. The ability to get somebody to do something – for good or bad – through nothing more than your ability to converse is indeed a skill we often miss, or at the very least take for granted. Yet the benefits of good communication are there to be seen. For example, Glennon (2010) notes that effective communication, generally means that you will be successful in your role, the converse is also true. Poor communication means that citizen complaints are higher, officers have greater amounts of time off with stress and feel less affinity for the organization and those they work with. Good communicators become more effective at the job. They know the neighborhood and community better than ever before, which in turn provides for an increased (mutual) respect as people are able to put a face to the service. As a consequence it can be expected that the day-to-day job would become safer, as greater interaction provides for greater opportunity to learn about activities in advance, thus enabling the officer (and their team) to better prepare.

Supporting a Positive Public

Supporting the public in local communities does not have to be expensive, nor does it have to be overly complicated. In a recent examination of non-emergency services in England and Wales, Bain et al. (2016) noted that the constant (and increasing) pressures placed upon already limited emergency service can be bolstered by the addition of a non-emergency service which can take a number of distinct roles and responsibilities. In part, the addition of part-time, and voluntary officers, could help to support police departments. Invariably members of the public want to know that they are being listened to, and taken seriously, and that even when the seriousness of the incident is in question they are still seen to be a priority.

In the United Kingdom good use has been made of the PCSOs (Police Community Support Officer) to fulfill this role, although they often lack the full range of training and arrest powers provided for in other areas. In the United States reserve officers are similarly used (although some agencies shy away from their use), providing additional services and security details which does not take away from the full-time commissioned officers, but can add to and support the work of the police department. However, as Wyllie (2011), has pointed out support for such officers will fall into one of two camps – for and/or against the use of part-time, reserve, and non-commissioned officers.

Those against the use of such officers (which could be referred to as auxiliary officers) often point to the fact that if this was not an option then more full-time officers would have to be employed to fill the gaps. This argument is evidentially flawed however, as it does not account for the ever increasing constraints placed upon budgets, or the fact that few in the general population would willingly increase their taxes to cover the additional costs of training, equipment, salaries, and benefits, needed to attract officers in the first place – hence the gaps which already exist in the service. An alternative maybe to draw from the ranks of law enforcement academies and local colleges/universities. Never forget, these individuals have already made the commitment and planned a career with the service, so their introduction to the community they are already part of, would seem to make good sense – as well as providing them with the professional practice. The use of college students would also provide for well-educated individuals with a clear understanding of the role, but lacking in the experience. I will note that there are some excellent internship programs out there, but many more lack a formal platform or structure, which leaves this resource completely untapped.

To a degree this is little more than formalizing the services, yet it may provide for a more dedicated and educated reserve force, and would undoubtedly go some way to supporting the image of officers on the street (Bain et al. 2014). In addition, it may also go some way to improving the relationship with community members. Bear and Reiken (2012) argue that whilst there exists a drive toward higher educational standards (in all walks of life), it is not necessarily the qualification that makes the greatest difference in law enforcement, but the ability of the individual officer to communicate, and provide a positive interaction with a local community. This may also go some way to combating the recent developments in policing which have tended to lead to reactive policing strategies rather than pro-active policing (as noted by Wentz and Schlimgen's 2012). The traditional image of officers walking around a local neighborhood can provide an excellent source of visibility and public relations, and even when evaluations of foot patrols have not provided evidence of a reduction in crime, they have helped nurture mutual respect and support between the service and community (Gaarder et al. 2004). Hall (2013) concurs, and has suggested that the positive impact that these [auxiliary] officers have on public perceptions cannot be denied.

When Things Are Not so Good

Conversely, however, when the perception is that the police (law enforcement) officer is there to manage, or babysit the community, then the relationship can quickly deteriorate. For example, Mazerolle et al. (2013) have noted that if the policing agency is acting in a fair way, then the public will see them as a legitimate source of authority, but when the perception is reversed and the police are seen as being unjust, or acting in a manner perceived as being over-bearing or heavy-handed, then public support is quickly withdrawn (Bain et al. 2014). Barker et al. (2008), add that the resulting outcome is a lack of trust in the local community which can see a portion of the public refuse to work with the police, therefore hindering any efforts to combat the criminal element in the local neighborhood/community. This maybe a reaction to similarly recognized cues which the officer uses to assess the situation when they first arrive at the scene, and can be based upon very little evidence other than the information provided by dispatch, and their own personal (prior) experience. However, in doing so the relationship is already hindered and may struggle to recover.

People are naturally attentive to the justice of events and situations in their everyday lives, across a variety of contexts, and for good reason – as they try to situate themselves within the context, or interpret meaning (Tabibnia et al. 2008). Thus, individuals react to actions and decisions made by organizations every day, some are seen to be positive others not so. Indeed, following the same argument of Tabibnia et al. (2008), an individual's perceptions of these decisions as fair or unfair can influence that person's subsequent attitudes and behaviors. Therefore, greatest concern arises for organizations (public and private) when the perceptions of injustice impact attitudes and behaviors of the individual and/or community, which carry their own consequence for the service provided.

Examples of this can be seen in the persistent use of video cameras and smartphones, recording the actions taken by officers at the scene. In part this maybe a natural reaction based upon a number of poorly handled incidence which have resulted in the harm, injury or in the worst case scenarios, the death of a suspect. These are unfortunate events, with devastating consequences but as is often the case, the video camera only captures one perspective and has a limited view (Ferrell 2013). Often times, it will only capture the point at which force is being used and does not record the prior altercation or attempts to resist by the suspect, thus losing context.

I am not acting as an apologist here, merely stating the same argument made time and again. An officer may have only one or two seconds to assess the situation, and make a decision which may result in harm or injury to themselves or others, and in those instances the use of body-worn cameras can make a great deal of difference to the inquiry (see Chapter 6 by Conser and Carsone in this text for a complete discussion of the use of body-worn cameras). However, it is the other cases, in which a suspect is fleeing or is none resistant which cause the greatest concern and have plagued the actions of officers in recent years. Indeed, Ferrell (2013) has noted that where there is a full video offered by the department (hopefully with audio as well as visual imaging) litigation involving law enforcement action can be overcome, and oftentimes there will be no case to answer. It is where the video evidence does not exist, or when the only video comes from the victim or a witness when the circumstances may not present themselves in a positive manner. We cannot prevent the recording from taking place, and nor should we try, to do so would only raise more questions and cast greater doubt upon the actions of the officer (never mind references made to the freedoms of speech, freedom of information, freedom to petition, and even the right to fair and equal justice – each of which reach far beyond the borders of North America). In addition, the argument can be made, that if the officer is acting within the boundaries of the law then the question of bystander video is irrelevant. This then brings us full cycle and back to the notion of technology and policing, communication and the community.

Summary: Understanding the Use of Electronic Technology

As was noted above – and should be evident – whatever technologies the police make use of, so to do the general public, whether offenders or not. The goal then is to make use of whichever technologies are available to best support the role of the officer and to present the community with the best information available. Further to this, Nuth (2008: 437) reminds us that "advancement in the field of Information Communication Technologies (ICTs) changes not only our society but also crime." Thus a good understanding, and general use, of ICTs will provide the individual officer with a better capacity for understanding the criminal behavior, and creates a race to understand the technology, but also raises significant concerns about the abuses of such technology.

Craven (2009) has noted that technology has evolved such that officers are no longer tied to their patrol cars for radio access and computer services, but are able to interact with people on a one-to-one basis as they did when policing was first professionalized. It may seem a strange – if not an awkward idea – but, as noted previously, when officers take the time to walk a part of the beat they get to see things that can easily be missed, or misunderstood, whilst in the relative comfort of their patrol car. Most language is never spoken; in fact Navarro (2008) has noted that 60–65% of all interpersonal communication is made up of non-verbal communication. Knowing these cues is perhaps as important as knowing the person. This is similarly espoused as part of the Reid (Interview) Technique put to good use today, both in private industry and criminal justice agencies. The act or action presented in response to questioning, may provide vital information which can easily be missed in other circumstances.

Furthermore, we often forget that the way we act, our body language, the things we say – and the ways in which we say them – all have an impact upon what people think (how they perceive us) and how they are likely to react to us in the future. Barker et al. (2008: para 2) make a good point, stating that by the very nature of their work "police officers communicate with people from a wide variety of backgrounds, attitudes, and preconceptions," every day. How they assess the situation and thus communicate with the individual, may have a great bearing upon how that person views the interaction and behaves from that point forward. This is supported by Schneider (1999) who has noted that there is a failure in community policing, because there is also a failure to recognize the divide which exists between the stated meaning and the assumed meaning – which are rarely the same thing. Key to this is an individual's ability to effectively communicate a requirement, a request, or an action, in plain and simple language.

This simplicity is often missed, but can be the most effective form of communication. Smile, speak in a clear and respectful manner and provide answers to any and all questions which arise. The results maybe an increased awareness of your surroundings, but will certainly provide for an increased level of respect between the two parties. The arising outcome may also be a more supportive and engaged community, and provide the catalyst for positive action on behalf of both parties – something which Robinson will consider in the next chapter, as he looks to explain the use of social media (by the general public and law enforcement agencies) today and what this may hold for building strategies for the future.

NOTES

1. Childs (1987) Inspector Morse.
2. Bruckheimer (2002) CSI Miami.
3. Coveny and Baldwin (2012) Longmire.
4. White (2014) Gotham.
5. Siegel (1971) Dirty Harry.
6. Swinden (2010) Luther.
7. Yost (2010) Justified For full academic source please see the reference list at the end of the chapter.

REFERENCES

Bain, A., Brooks, G., Golding, B., Ellis, T., & Lewis, C. (2016). Calling the police: The use of non-emergency 101 in England and Wales. *The Police Journal: Theory, Practice and Principles, 89*, 1–15.

Bain, A., Robinson, B. K., & Conser, J. (2014). Perceptions of policing: Improving communication in local communities. *International Journal of Police, Science & Management, 16*(4), 267–276.

Barker, V., Giles, H., Hajek, C., Ota, H., Noels, K., Lim, T.-S., & Somera, L. (2008). Police communication. Why does it matter? *Communication Currents, 3*(3). Available at: https://www.natcom.org/CommCurrentsArticle.aspx?id=886.

Bear, D., & Reiken, J. (2012, March 24). Should all police officers really be university-educated? *The Guardian.* Available at: http://www.theguardian.com/commentisfree/2012/mar/24/police-officers-university-education.

Bernstein, B. (1961). Social class and linguistic development – A theory of social learning. In A. H. Halsey, J. Floud, & C. A. Anderson (Eds.), *Education, economy and society.* New York: Free Press.

Bernstein, B. (1971). *Class, codes and control.* (Vol. 1). London: Routledge.

Bernstein, B. (1990). *The structuring of pedagogic discourse – Class, codes and control.* (Vol. 4). London: Routledge.

Bruckheimer, J. (Producer). (2002). *CSI Miami [Television Series].* Fairfax, Los Angeles, CA: CBS Television Network.

Childs, T. (Producer). (1987). *Morse [Television Series].* Birmingham, UK: Zenith Productions – Central Independent Television.

Coveny, J., & Baldwin, H. (Producers). (2012). *Longmire [Television Series].* Burbank (CA): Warner Horizon Television.

Craven, K. (2009, February). Foot patrols: Crime analysis and community engagement to further the commitment to community policing. *Community Policing Dispatch, 2*(2). Available at: http://cops.usdoj.gov/html/dispatch/February_2009/foot_patrol.htm.

Doyle, M. (2014, March). Cell phones on duty. *Police: The Law Enforcement Magazine.* Available at: http://www.policemag.com/channel/technology/articles/2014/03/cell-phones-on-duty.aspx.

Estey, J. G. (2005, April). The presidents message: Communication is critical to law enforcement. *The Police Chief, 72*(3). Available at: http://www.policechiefmagazine.org/magazine/index.cfm?fuseaction=display_arch&article_id=561&issue_id=42005.

Ferrell, C. E. (2013 October). The future is here: How police officers' videos protect officers and departments. *The Police Chief, 80*, 16–18. Available at: http://www.policechiefmagazine.org/magazine/index.cfm?fuseaction=display_arch&article_id=3139&issue_id=102013.

Gaarder, E., Rodriguez, N., & Zatz, M. (2004). Criers, liars, and manipulators: Probation officers' views of girls. *Justice Quarterly, 21*, 547–578.

Glennon, J. (2010, February 22). Communication skills and your survival. *PoliceOne.com*. Available at: https://www.policeone.com/patrol-issues/articles/2008039-Communication-skills-and-your-survival/.

Greer, C., & Reiner, R. (2012). Mediated Mayhem: Media, crime, criminal justice. In M. Maguire, R. Morgan, & R. Reiner (Eds.), *The Oxford handbook of criminology* (5th ed.). Oxford: Oxford University Press.

Hall, M. (2013). Bobbies on the beat could become an endangered species, police association head warns. *The Independent*. Available at: http://www.telegraph.co.uk/news/uknews/law-and-order/10294708/Bobbies-on-the-beat-could-become-an-endangered-species-police-association-head-warns.html.

Herbst, L., & Walker, S. (2001). Language barriers in the delivery of police services. A study of police and Hispanic interactions in a midwestern city. *Journal of Criminal Justice, 29*, 329–340.

Kelling, G. L., & Moore, M. H. (1988 November). *The evolving strategy of policing.* Perspectives on Policing, No. 4. Washington, DC: National Institute of Justice.

Mazerolle, L., Antrobus, E., Bennett, S., & Tyler, T. (2013). Shaping citizen perception of police legitimacy: A randomized field trial of procedural justice. *Criminology, 51*(1), 33–64.

Navarro, J. (2008). *What every body is saying*. New York, NY: Harper.

Nuth, M. S. (2008). Taking advantage of new technologies: For and against crime. *Computer Law & Security Report, 28*, 437–446.

Police Staff. (2005, December 1). Does community policing work? *Police: The Law Enforcement Magazine*. Available at: http://www.policemag.com/channel/patrol/articles/2005/12/does-community-policing-work.aspx.

Schneider, S. (1999). Overcoming barriers to communication between police and socially disadvantaged neighborhoods: A critical theory of community policing. *Crime, Law & Social Change, 30*, 347–377.

Siegel, D. (Producer & Director). (1971). *Dirty Harry [Motion Picture]*. Burbank, CA: Malpaso Productions.

Swinden, K. (Producer). (2010). *Luther [Television Series]*. London, UK: BBC Drama Productions.

Tabibnia, G., Satpute, A., & Lieberman, M. (2008). The sunny side of fairness: Preference for fairness activities reward circuitry (and disregarding fairness activates self-control circuitry). *Psychological Science, 19*(4), 339–347.

Tooley, M., Linkenbach, J., Lande, B. J., & Lande, G. M. (2009). Media, the public, and the law enforcement community: Correcting misperceptions. *The Police Chief, 76*(6), 62–67.

Wentz, E., & Schlimgen, K. (2012). Citizens' perceptions of police service and police response to community concerns. *Journal of Crime and Justice, 35*, 114–133.

White, S. (Producer). (2014). *Gotham [Television Series]*. Burbank, CA: Warner Bros.

Wyllie, D., (2011). The reserve officer's role in law enforcement. *PoliceOne.com*. Available at: https://www.policeone.com/patrol-issues/articles/4239138-The-reserve-officers-role-in-law-enforcement/.

Yost, G. (Producer). (2010). *Justified [Television Series]*. Los Angeles, CA: FX Productions.

Andy Bain is Assistant Professor of Criminal Justice at the University of Mount Union, Ohio, USA. He holds a PhD in Offender Behavior, a MSc in Criminal Justice, and a Graduate Diploma in Psychology. Andy is the coauthor of *Outlaw Motorcycle Gangs: A Theoretical Perspective* (with Mark Lauchs & Peter Bell), and previously coauthored *Professional Risk Taking with People: A Guide to Decision-Making in Health, Social Care & Criminal Justice* (with David Carson). In addition Andy has published in a number of leading international academic and professional journals. His professional background includes 4 years with the National Probation Service (England & Wales) and 6 years running a successful criminal justice consultancy group, providing guidance and advice to offender groups, law enforcement agencies and correctional bodies. This, in turn led to the publication of a number of local and national policing and corrections reports. He is an active member of national and international professional bodies, and his research interests include tattoo and culture, gangs and coded language; policing and social groups; social-psychology of offending and risk-taking behavior; and the (psychological) investigation of criminal behavior.

CHAPTER 5

Technology at Work: Attitudes Toward Law Enforcement in "Social" Media

Bryan K. Robinson

Abstract This chapter examines community attitudes toward local law enforcement through the lens of social media reports. Content analysis of 301 online reviews of police stations from Los Angeles, Chicago, Houston, and Philadelphia are used to illustrate common themes in public opinions of the police. It is suggested that further investigation into the benefits and harms of social media may assist public relations efforts by police agencies. As a relatively young technology that has profoundly impacted everyday life it is important that both researchers and law enforcement alike begin to come to terms with the power of social media and its impact on law enforcement.

Keywords Social media · Public opinion · Online reviews · Internet

INTRODUCTION

In the modern era of hyper-connectivity, one individual's opinion can be shared instantly and solidified into the public record with little more than a few taps of a thumb on a cell phone screen. In fact, recent studies have

B.K. Robinson (✉)
Department of Sociology and Criminal Justice, University of Mount Union, Alliance, OH, USA
e-mail: robinsbk@mountunion.edu

© The Author(s) 2016
A. Bain (ed.), *Law Enforcement and Technology*,
DOI 10.1057/978-1-137-57915-7_5

63

confirmed the near market saturation of social media technologies among virtually all demographics in America (Perrin 2015; Pew Research Center 2015). As smartphone technologies proliferate, they are weaving a vast mobile network that can have a magnification effect on social attitudes by amplifying the opinions or experiences of an individual as they spread across the network.

Ever since the Rodney King incident in 1991, the law enforcement community has found itself operating under the watchful eye of a community with an increasing power to disseminate its observations and judgments with lightning speed and a global reach. Over the past year, the presence of cell phones and social media networks have shone a spotlight on the interactions of police in the community, both good and bad, as citizens post live video and comments directly to the world-wide web. The Black Lives Matter movement is a good example of how the presence of these new technologies can vastly impact policing routines, tactics, and policies at both the local and national level. Ever since the "#blacklifesmatter" appeared in the wake of the Trayvon Martin shooting, activists have used social media outlets to rally support and mobilize protesters in response to concerns about police conduct and societal reactions in general to incidents of African Americans who have died in encounters with police (Stephen 2015). The new technologies' ability to get the word out and to act as an ever-present recorder of police and civilian behavior has brought a level of transparency and accountability to everyday life that has both challenged and assisted the police in recent years. Given the rapid proliferation of information distribution technologies (i.e. cell phones) and information distribution platforms (e.g. Twitter, Facebook, Tumblr, Yik Yak, etc.), it is essential to begin considering how these modern tools are being used by the community to characterize the men and women who serve and protect their neighborhoods.

Prior research on public opinions of law enforcement has primarily examined legacy media outlets such as television, radio, and newsprint while largely ignoring the emerging influence of social media applications and websites. We have learned, however, from these studies that media coverage of perceived police misconduct can have profound negative impacts on public opinion (Weitzer 2002). We have also learned that crime-related television can improve the viewer's perception of police assuming that the viewer has no prior contact with law enforcement as a victim or offender (Callanan and Rosenberger 2011). But these studies only show the one-directional effect of traditional media. To better understand the interactive nature of social media, we can look at research on word-of-mouth on perceptions of law enforcement. Studies examining this question find that negative perceptions of police are often rooted in personal negative experiences of those with regular police contact (Carr et al. 2007), but both positive and negative perceptions can be influenced by indirect or vicarious experiences for many individuals (Rosenbaum et al. 2005).

Given the potential benefits and the risk of digital publicity coupled with the ability of social media to act as both a source of traditional media information and a form of word-of-mouth communication, it is worth taking the time to explore how law enforcement is portrayed via this relatively young technology. It is also worth looking at departmental websites which thus far have served as the primary digital presence for many law enforcement agencies. In contrast to the Milwaukee, WI, police department (http://www.milwaukeepolicenews.com/), few official police department websites are designed to be effective marketing tools to advertise the police and combat negative publicity. Consequently, most police departments' web presence appears as an afterthought, at best, as many agencies simply have nothing more than a city or county government-supplied template that provides only minimal information and does little to draw the general public's attention.

Although many different social media outlets exist, few are as universally available and easily accessible as the review function on Google Maps. Neilson ratings (2014) places Google Maps as the fifth most widely used smartphone app of 2014 in the United States. Furthermore, given Google's dominance as a search engine, it is easy to imagine that many users might also use its review function to both post and read reviews. Actually, the idea for this chapter developed out of a routine Google Maps search made on a smartphone while trying to navigate from a conference hotel to a nearby precinct station for a police ride-along. That search led to about a dozen reviews of the local police station, and those reviews spawned a deeper curiosity about the role of social media in public opinion of the police.

How Can We Assess the Public's Attitude toward Law Enforcement?

Given that we have previously noted that little evidence exists in this area, what does this tell us about the public and local law enforcement departments and the ways in which policing is viewed in those local communities? Public perception and understanding of policing routines – as discussed by

Bain in the previous chapter – is undoubtedly an area of great concern, and something which can help, as easily as hinder, the work of local forces/ departments.

In preparation for this chapter, and in the absence of specific work, I took the opportunity to conduct an impromptu examination of a number of police departments in the United States, and looked at the comments left by members of the public, in response to the encounters they had with the local officers. To do this, I analyzed the reviews posted to Google Map searches of urban police stations in four major cities. The present chapter investigates community perceptions of law enforcement by analyzing user reviews posted to Google Maps searches of urban police stations in those same U.S. cities. This study focuses on all reviews posted during the 36 months prior to July 2014 for police stations located in four of the five most populous American cities: Los Angeles (CA), Chicago (IL), Houston (TX), and Philadelphia (PA). These cities were chosen in order to maximize the geographic dispersal of the department reviews and to target areas with high enough population densities to insure a sufficient number of reviews.

When someone searches for a police station, Google Maps can provide not only directions but an overview of the ratings that precinct has received including the total number of reviewers and the average number of stars assigned by those reviewers. These star ratings, which range from one to five with more stars representing better reviews, are easily recognizable to most users since many consumer review systems use them to indicate overall quality of service. Police stations in Los Angeles, the second most populous city in America, garnered 63 reviews with a 2.95-star average rating. Chicago, the third most populous city, had 54 reviews for its police stations with a 3.26-star average rating. Houston ranks fourth in overall population, and its police departments had 38 reviews and 2.61-star average rating. Finally, Philadelphia, the fifth most populous city, had the most ratings, 146, and the worst overall with a 1.28-star rating. Once gathered, the 301 reviews were grouped by the number of stars the reviewer assigned and then examined for themes and trends. Table 5.1 provides a breakdown of the reviews by rating.

It is worth noting that the overwhelming majority of reviewers scored the police either five stars (24.6%) or one star (61.5%). This seems to imply that only very happy or very disappointed individuals took the time to review the police. This U-shaped relationship within the reviews is, however, expected given prior research on common distributions of positive

Table 5.1 Total number of reviews and total number of comments by number of stars assigned

	Total	*With comments*
5-star reviews	74	32
4-star reviews	9	9
3-star reviews	6	4
2-star reviews	27	18
1-star reviews	185	169

and negative reviews (E. W. Anderson 1998), so as with restaurants: you only hear from the happiest and maddest of customers. It should also be noted that roughly one-third of the reviews provided ranking only and did not contain any comments, and that about a dozen or so of the reviews were nonsensical or written in a language other than English, making them difficult to interpret for the majority of the population.

WHAT IS THE SOCIAL MEDIA TELLING US ABOUT THE POLICE?

In order to best make sense of the 301 reviews, we can start looking at the more favorable postings and then work down through the less favorable ones. This approach will allow for a natural progression from the accolades to the concerns, and perhaps offer some sense of community concern and how we should approach these areas.

High Praise

Among the four- and five-star evaluations, the general trend focused on personal experiences that reflected an appreciation of law enforcement as problem solvers, mediators, and service providers. An example of a typical five star review reflecting these qualities is:

Excellent police department! Public service at its finest. My car was in a hit and run and not in operating condition. I'm not a mechanic but I could tell the frame was bent by at least 1.5 feet away from what it used to be rendering it inoperable. Upon contacting the police department they indicated to come in the station and I told them I had no ride since my car doesn't work anymore and am about 5 miles away. After waiting approximately 3.5 hours a police officer showed up and wrote a report. I think they should get all their raises and a bonus for fine police work! Stop cutting resources to the Chicago Police Department!

Many of the personal narratives in these reviews reflected on the customer service aspects of the citizen/police relationship. These personal stories also represented not only the experiences of victims seeking assistance but also, surprisingly, the experiences of offenders. In the former, case reviewers spoke highly of officers responding to events like robberies and auto accidents, while in the latter, case reviewers wrote of officers who defused violent situations or helped them get back on track with their lives. One such reviewer wrote, "*High tension, but both officers helped me keep my cool amidst provocation. Also kept me from stepping into the incident more deeply with wise counsel. Thanks.*" Other examples of this type of praise came in the form of reviewers who expressed admiration for the professionalism of the officers who stopped them and those officers' dedication to the community. The focus on community service can also be seen in reviews posted in response to how helpful officers were with giving directions, or setting up traffic detours during power outages. In general, these postings show how community-oriented policing draws positive responses from all types of community members, in a similar way to how the importance attached to communication with the community can influence perceptions of legitimacy and fairness in policing (see Bain et al. 2014).

Further evidence of the public perception of legitimacy in community policing is an interesting trend among the higher rated reviews to personally identify officers who the reviewer felt went above and beyond. Two good examples of this include a reviewer who wrote: "*Thank you to Officer Diaz. He found my wallet that I dropped at a service staton [sic]. He returned it to my hotel and called me. I could not believe my luck that a Policeman found it.*" Another reviewer who appears to be disappointed with the police in general still felt the need to show appreciation for two specific officers. "*I have to honestly say not all cops are bad at the 6th district there are 2 officers who should be honered [sic] for their hard work officers Rose and Riddick. If all cops were like them there would be less crime on the streets.*" While naming specific officers was popular in the positive reviews, a few of the negative reviews named specific officers as well. The one thing that many of the reviews naming an individual had in common was a reference to repeat contact with that officer.

Middle of the Road Evaluations

Three stars was the rarest of all reviews, with only six of the reviewers issuing this score and only four of these reviews included comments one per city. Unfortunately, these four comments provide little in the way of constructive criticism, but it is interesting to list them here:

- "Free room for the night if you're misbehavin' LOL!"
- "Please ban parking in front of super kings recieving area on s mission it It is a hazard and dangerous in the morning. To many truckers trying to get around in that area" [*sic*].
- "A nice place to pray to the Almighty."
- "ok"

What these reviews do provide is a glimpse of some of the more pointless, poetic, and/or philosophical statements that were peppered throughout the reviews. They are also a helpful reminder that these online reviews are often like graffiti which can be difficult to understand or interpret when observed out of context.

Poor Opinions

Turning to the more negative reviews, most of the two-star comments can be divided into complaints about communication and/or complaints about trust. Communication complaints often focused on difficulties with making initial contact with the station. For example, one exasperated reviewer wrote: "*No answer at all. Kind of ridiculous*" while another echoed: "*This does not appear to be the correct phone number, or they never answer it.*" Complaints of this nature are interesting because it is unclear as to why these individuals are unable to contact the station. These by in large are attempts to contact the station directly and not by using 911 emergency services, but it is clearly a source of disappointment and frustration when these attempts fail.

> I just discovered my car was stolen, so I phoned this district office. It's like trying to call Macy's toy dept. at Christmas; is there no one on duty to handle incoming calls? It's obviously not of importance to them; not even the courtesy of a recorded message. It rings interminably then switches to a busy signal.

These statements and dozens of others show an obvious expectation by civilians that the listed phone number for police stations will be accurate and answered just as they would expect from any other business. Moreover, reviewers expressed similar concerns with automated answer systems used by some of the stations. *"Could you list your open hours of operation for office hours as well as phone assistance? Your automated system is not helpful and errors."* Once again, these complaints seem to mirror the frustration consumers feel with customer support provided by many retail and service industries. Other two-star reviewers complained about the lack of customer service skills as well as the response time of officers:

> I asked a simple question and this police offic [*sic*] guy caught an attitude for no reason, they say that they're here to serve and protect. I don't think so then they take forever to come to your rescue like your situation isn't important to them.

In a similar vein, other reviewers took offense with what they saw as a lack of customer service and described their encounters with officers using terms like: "rude," "racist," "arrogant," and "lazy." These should all be of great concern given expectations of professionalism that the community has for law enforcement officers.

The notion of not being taken seriously was repeated in several of the negative reviews as well.

> Called for loud music/noise disturbance after 1:00 am. One and a half hours later the music was till [*sic*] going strong and LA's finest (definite sarcasm) were nowhere to be found. Whether they ever showed up or the party simply ended at almost 3:00 am is unknown.

One of the difficulties with complaints about response times is that they often don't take into account the other more pressing calls that police may be responding to. Consequently, an upset caller with a noise complaint probably has no clue as to whether the police are ignoring the call out of laziness or because they are too busy dealing with a more serious incident such as a robbery or car wreck. However, the negative reaction by the caller shows a need for finding more avenues for communicating response times to citizens calling in complaints.

Distrust of local police and the police in general was also present in many of the negative reviews. General distrust of law enforcement can be seen in comments like: "*They are here to rob people of their liberty!! That's all!!*" Distrust of local police also appeared in comments reflecting race concerns: "*They are some white racist cops here… don't be black driving*" "*through there district!!!!! BEWARE!!!!!*" and comments in response to specific incidents:

LET'S GET ONE THING CRYSTAL CLEAR. AS LONG AS I AM NOT COMMITTING A CRIME, AIDING AND ABETTING A CRIMINAL OR INTERFERING WITH ANY POLICE OFFICER IN THE PROCESS OF PERFORMING THEIR "OFFICIAL" DUTIES, I REFUSE TO BE HARASSED AND THREATENED BY A THUG PARADING AS A LAW ABIDING CHICAGO POLICE OFFICER. AS A CITIZEN OF THIS CITY AND STATE, REGARDLESS OF HOW CORRUPT IT'S POLICE DEPARTMENTS ARE, I WILL GO ANY DAMN WHERE I PLEASE!! THIS STATEMENT IS DIRECTED TO THE 3RD DIST. CPD BECAUSE I WAS THREATENED IN THE 3RD DISTRICT BY 3RD DIST. THUGS PARADING AS POLICE OFFICERS.

At the low end of the scale, the one-star reviews appear to take one of three approaches. First, a large number of the comments were simply insults with little explanation for their ire. Still others seemed to appeal solely to the media as their source of information on the police. Finally, others focused on intensely negative personal experiences with law enforcement.

General Angst

Among the one-star reviews focused on general angst, there were a number of attempts to compare law enforcement to organized crime: "*Extremely crooked, like a gang,*" wrote one reviewer while another wrote: "*Mobsters in uniform…*" Still another wrote: "*Criminals with badges!*" Beyond the criminal gang analogy were several complaints comparing cops to school yard bullies. Reviewers wrote things like: "*Bullies with badges. Watch their videos for proof,*" and "*Please stop harming taxpayers who pay you lowlife bullies for protection!*" While little evidence or logic was supplied in most of these style comments, the sentiment is clear that the police are not trusted as whole. One reviewer went so far as to argue that gangs were preferable to the police:

Only the most naive amongst us would believe the fairy tales told by the always-lying Philadelphia cops. They are nothing more than a gang of criminal cowards who wear silly uniforms. I would trust ANY civilian gang more than Philly cops; at least the former have SOME honor and integrity!

This lack of trust and general contempt for law enforcement extended into attacks on other reviewers who had posted positive comments. One such reviewer wrote: "*Who is the dimwitted loser who gave these felons five stars? Pigs only help themselves, not taxpayers who pay them for protection.*" While another reviewer argued "*You actually gave five stars to these crooked cowards just because one of them helped you one time?*" Both of these reviews show the cohesive nature of online forums which can drown out positive reviews or drive the reviews off topic as reviewers engage in arguments that often stray from the topic at hand.

Media Fueled Distrust

Organizing the reviews by city as well as ratings draws attention to the fact that nearly half of all the reviews for Philadelphia were one-star reviews (see Table 5.2). Of particular interest among the one-star reviews from Philadelphia were a significant number of references to negative media coverage focused on corruption.

Clearly drawing upon the media reports, one reviewer attempted to rally others against the police by writing: "*If you have recently read the Daily News, you may have much less respect for police officers.*" While many other reviewers echoed this concern, based on what they saw in the media, few made references to old school media (e.g. TV, newspapers, radio, etc.). In fact, most focused on online sources: "*Even Amnesty International has implied that Philadelphia's police officers are the nation's most criminal. To discover why, Google the video 'Philly Cops: Felons With Badges.'*" Moreover, 18% of all the reviews written about the Philadelphia police mentioned the

Table 5.2   Number of stars assigned by city

	5 stars	4 stars	3 stars	2 stars	1 star	Total
Los Angeles	26	1	2	12	22	63
Chicago	25	4	1	8	16	54
Houston	12	2	2	3	19	38
Philadelphia	11	1	1	4	129	146

Wikipedia page on Philadelphia police corruption specifically. One example cited both the Wikipedia page and a 60 Minutes special:

> Philadelphia is the proud owner of the world's only police force that has a Wikipedia misconduct page that is updated daily. As Officer Ron Previte stated in his "60 Minutes" interview, "most" Philadelphia police officers belong in jail.

Other reviews simply referred to the Wikipedia page by imploring others to: "*search 'Wikipedia', then 'misconduct in the Philadelphia police department'. If you're still a fan after visiting that site, you should have your head examined.*"

The fact that so many of the online negative reviews referenced the media and that one Wikipedia page in particular show the magnification effect that social media can have. Nearly 20% of all the one-star reviews received by Philadelphia police precincts reference the Wikipedia page; by contrast, only 2% of their one-star reviews reference personal experiences with the police. The significantly higher proportion of reviews for Philadelphia are partially accounted for by individuals who are echoing what they have read on other social media sites.

As a point of comparison, a quick review of the agencies' websites provide evidence for many of these themes as some of the concerns and accolades in the reviews appear to be echoed in the content of the sites. Chicago, for example, received some of the highest praise and was the only agency to offer a simple and easy way to log compliments or complaints against officers from their homepage. Moreover, Chicago's Police Department website spoke often about serving the community and community concerns while Philadelphia, the poorest ranked of the four agencies, focused its website on recruitment and ways for the citizens to help the police. Although the website for Philadelphia's police force is not significantly different than any other police website in America, it doesn't provide any assurance that the focus is on community and service and instead focuses on the fraternal nature of law enforcement, which does little to counter the criticisms of the media and the reviewers. Given the larger number of negative reviews in Philadelphia and their link to media-driven publicity, it is worth considering that some agencies may be losing the public relations battle by failing to adequately engage both the traditional media and social media.

Personal Accounts

In a strange twist from the high number of negative reviews in Philadelphia that referenced the media, the other three cities examined saw mostly personal stories in their one-star reviews. While only 2% of the one-star comments in Philadelphia made any reference to a personal experience, all of Chicago's, two thirds of Los Angeles, and roughly half of Houston's did. Another particularly perplexing trend is the lack of real detail in personal stories among the dissatisfied posters. Although five-star and four-star posters often gave some detail as to what led to their praise, the typical one-star post gave vague accusations at best. For example, one reviewer wrote: "*These so called policemen robbed me.*" While another complained: "*Been treated in such a rude way, for no reason.*" In fact, it was a common thread for many of these reviewers to insist that they had in no way provoked the mistreatment by police: "*Very very very very rude and disrespectful fit no damn reason at all... Liars! Wish I could've rated NO STARS AT ALL!:-(.*" Despite the majority of these reviews lacking specific details there were a few that provided some detail such as: "*Unhelpful completely. You get rerouted for 5 hours, find your friend's clothes shredded by police canines and still no one knows where they are. Currently 6 hours in.*" Occasionally the reviews turned graphic in language and at times began to resemble bathroom graffiti as one reviewer wrote: "*two pigs arrested me for smoking a joint. One was an absolute as whole moron with the mentality of a 12 year old. SUCK MY DiICK, PIGS*" [*sic*]. While such reviews are easily dismissed as sophomoric, it is important to realize that, as with graffiti, these visceral rants might be indicative of deeper community sentiments toward the police and early warnings of public unrest like the clashes with police that followed the Rodney King verdict in 1992 and Freddie Gray's death in 2014.

SUMMARY: MOVING FORWARD

While little documentation exists on the effects of online reviews, some research indicates that both the service industry (Sparks and Browning 2011) and retail market (Chintagunta et al. 2010) can be influenced by these reviews. Moreover, research has identified a clear link between online review and perceived trustworthiness of various industries (Utz et al. 2012) as well as a link between negative reviews and future success of some industries (Chintagunta et al. 2010).

At first glance, it may seem strange to assume marketing data for hotels and online stores could in any way inform us about the relationship between citizens and police, but it is worth considering given that emergency services are indeed services to the community. It is also important to keep in mind that, as with retail services, citizens can and sometimes do choose alternatives when trust levels are too low. For example, the southern subcultural theory of violence rests on the premise that disenfranchised Southerners are more likely than Northerners to take legal matters into their own hands in the form of self-defense, vigilantism, and mob justice (Corzine et al. 1999). The shooting of Trayvon Martin by George Zimmerman is a good example of self-help citizen policing gone wrong. Similarly, research on urban culture has also noted that

> Feeling that they cannot depend on the police and other civil authorities to protect them from danger, residents often take personal responsibility for their security...And they tend to teach their children to stand up for themselves physically or to meet violence with violence
>
> Anderson 1999: 109

Anderson's description is further echoed in the interviews conducted by Carr et al. (2007) with inter-city youth in Philadelphia. Moreover, just because local law enforcement may be the only game in town when it comes to calling for help it does not mean that distrustful citizens won't further complicate the job of officers by refusing to cooperate or becoming hostile during routine interactions. As Charles Derber (2015) recently warned, the combination of an armed citizenry, distrust for government services, and broadly defined self-defense laws are all combining into a recipe for disaster as routine street interactions quickly devolve into Wild West style confrontations. Given the tragic outcomes of the 1992 Los Angeles Riots in the wake of the Rodney King verdict as well as the 2015 Baltimore Protest following the death of Freddie Gray, it would be wise for law enforcement to give serious consideration to the concerns expressed by citizens via social media.

Policy-wise, law enforcement agencies need to be aware of the rapid replication of negative media content through social media. It is imperative that agencies consider the content of their own web presence and consider using social media as a tool to better reach out to the community at large. Agencies should also seriously weigh the fact that many members of the community expect customer service as part of the experience when they come in contact with the police. Specifically, professionalism, small courtesies, and open lines of communication all rate high on the concerns for the reviewers.

In order to better facilitate the discussion between citizens and police, it seems appropriate that academics, policy makers, and law enforcement officials should further explore the use of social media as a forum for public opinion regarding law enforcement. Many platforms exist to disseminate reports of police behavior in real time as well as expedite word-of-mouth opinions. But these tools could equally be leveraged by police to highlight the positive aspects of their work. For example, agencies could monitor social media for signs of discontent with police work and make reasonable changes based on reoccurring complaints. Moreover, agencies could employ social media tools by posting their own messages about successful arrests as well as community outreach projects.

References

Anderson, E. (1999). *Code of the street: Decency, violence, and the moral life of the inner city.* New York: W. W. Norton.

Anderson, E. W. (1998). Customer satisfaction and word of mouth. *Journal of Service Research, 1*(1), 5–17. doi: 10.1177/109467059800100102.

Bain, A., Robinson, B. K., & Conser, J. (2014). Perceptions of policing: Improving communication in local communities. *International Journal of Police Science & Management, 16*(4): 267–276.

Callanan, V. J., & Rosenberger, J. S. (2011). Media and public perceptions of the police: Examining the impact of race and personal experience. *Policing and Society, 21*(2), 167–189. doi: 10.1080/10439463.2010.540655.

Carr, P. J., Napolitano, L., & Keating, J. (2007). We never calll the cops and here is why: A qualitative examination of legal cynicism in three Philadelphia neighborhoods. *Criminology, 45*(2), 445–480. doi: 10.1111/j.1745-9125.2007.00084.x.

Chintagunta, P. K., Gopinath, S., & Venkataraman, S. (2010). The effects of online user reviews on movie box office performance: Accounting for sequential rollout and aggregation across local markets. *Marketing Science, 29*(5), 944–957. doi: 10.1287/mksc.1100.0572.

Corzine, J., Huff-Corzine, L., & Whitt, H. P. (1999). Cultural and subcultural theories of homicide. In M. D. Smith & M. A. Zahn (Eds.), *Homicide: A sourcebook of social research* (pp. 42–57). Thousand Oaks: Sage Publications.

Derber, C. (2015). *The wilding of America: Money, mayhem, and the new American dream.* New York: Worth.

Nielsen. (2014). Tops of 2014: Digital. Available at: http://www.nielsen.com/us/en/insights/news/2014/tops-of-2014-digital.html.

Perrin, A. (2015). Social networking usage: 2005–2015. Available at: http://www.pewinternet.org/2015/10/08/social-networking-usage-2005-2015/.

Pew Research Center. (2015). The smartphone difference. Available at: http://www.pewinternet.org/2015/04/01/us-smartphone-use-in-2015/.

Rosenbaum, D. P., Schuck, A. M., Costello, S. K., Hawkins, D. F., & Ring, M. K. (2005). Attitudes toward the police: The effects of direct and vicarious experience. *Police Quarterly, 8*(3), 343–365. doi: 10.1177/1098611104271085.

Sparks, B. A., & Browning, V. (2011). The impact of online reviews on hotel booking intentions and perception of trust. *Tourism Management, 32*(6), 1310–1323. doi: http://dx.doi.org/10.1016/j.tourman.2010.12.011.

Stephen, B. (2015). Social media helps black lives matter fight the power. *Wired, 23*, 120–121.

Utz, S., Kerkhof, P., & Van Den Bos, J. (2012). Consumers rule: How consumer reviews influence perceived trustworthiness of online stores. *Electronic Commerce Research and Applications, 11*(1), 49–58. doi: http://dx.doi.org/10.1016/j.elerap.2011.07.010.

Weitzer, R. (2002). Incidents of police misconduct and public opinion. *Journal of Criminal Justice, 30*(5), 397–408. doi: http://dx.doi.org/10.1016/S0047-2352(02)00150-2.

Bryan K. Robinson is a criminologist with research interest in lethal violence, criminological theory, and media depictions of crime. Bryan completed his doctoral degree in Sociology at the State University of New York, Albany in 2012. His dissertation examined the role of religious institutions on suicide and homicide rates in U.S. counties. His current research includes an analysis of census data and state corrections data to assess the effect of religious, family, and economic variables on county level recidivism rates. Bryan has published on Team-Based Learning Methods, media depictions of family life, and international research on teen suicide rates. He currently teaches a range of classes on the undergraduate program at the University of Mount Union (Ohio), which includes: Introduction to Sociology, Introduction to Criminology, Sociology of Violence, Media and Society, and Drugs and Society.

CHAPTER 6

Technology that Aids the Investigative Process

James A. Conser and Louis P. Carsone

Abstract Conser and Carsone describe the advancement and development of selected technologies in use for criminal investigations. Emphasis is placed on technologies related to communications, smartphone applications, patrol aids, crime scene analysis, surveillance, evidence processing, and crime laboratory equipment; primarily for their investigative potential. For example, today's investigators may obtain valuable information from social media, cell phones, video images from body-cams and other mobile devices, three-dimensional laser scanning of crime scenes, real-time crime analysis, touch DNA, and license plate readers. The chapter is concluded with a brief discussion of limitations, precautions, and policy implications.

Keywords Crime scene and investigative technologies · Policy issues

J.A. Conser (✉)
Department of Sociology and Criminal Justice, University of Mount Union, Alliance, OH, USA

Department of Criminal Justice and Forensic Science, Youngstown State University, Youngstown, OH, USA
e-mail: theconsers@frontier.com or jaconser@ysu.edu

L.P. Carsone
Department of Public Safety, Hubbard, OH, USA
e-mail: bluejet514@neo.rr.com

© The Author(s) 2016
A. Bain (ed.), *Law Enforcement and Technology*,
DOI 10.1057/978-1-137-57915-7_6

79

INTRODUCTION

Criminal investigators and patrol officers know that unless they have been an eyewitness to an offense, they are not going to "solve" that offense without obtaining the necessary information. The importance of *information* cannot be disputed in decisions to arrest, prosecute, and convict a subject. That information must be acquired through diligent, lawful, and relevant procedures; whether it is through basic interviewing, detailed canvassing, suspect interrogating, or sophisticated forensic science analysis. All law enforcement personnel are trained in initial criminal investigation procedures/practices when they attend their basic academy. As their careers progress, they learn new procedures and evolving technological aids.

The focus of this chapter is on how various technologies are capable of assisting with criminal investigations or incident documentation. Selected technological advances from the street to the crime lab are discussed in terms of the overall investigative process. It is not our purpose here to describe in detail the history and specifications of each technology used (which has already been addressed to some degree in Chapters 1 and 2), but rather to focus on how they assist in "solving the incident" or better documenting an event. The chapter describes several concerns and limitations about the deployment, implementation, and impact of such technologies on law enforcement agencies, from the perspective of individual officers to administrators. Policy implications and concerns are raised as well as the need for possible legislative reforms.

However, before moving to a discussion of technologies at the crime scene, it is worth taking just a few short paragraphs to acknowledge the work of technology today, and to perhaps, further contextualize some of the discussion which has taken place up to now. This may then provide some credence as to how and why we have chosen to focus the remainder of the chapter on specific equipment and technological advances.

COMMUNICATION

As Bain notes in Chapter 4, there is more to communication than just radio, telephone, and media; in fact there is some benefit to recognizing the use and impact of each to how we communicate our understanding to and of the community (a point made by Robinson in Chapter 5). Yet, the evolution from analogue phone and radio systems to the digital era, coupled with computer data storage capabilities, has meant that copious amounts of information are generated and stored. This information may be related to initial calls for assistance or to the historical record of phone usage of victims, witnesses, and suspects, and said information is now readily available. As cell phones become the majority device used to communicate with others, cell phone records and analysis play a more significant role in case analysis. Cell phones today are equivalent to computers in terms of the information they potentially contain: names and phone numbers of contacts, text messages, photos, video, GPS coordinates, web browsing history, call details, chat messages, and even deleted data can be retrieved for investigators.

Cell phones are essentially mini-computers and today's smartphones are capable of many functions beyond voice communication and data storage. Estimates from 2013 indicate there are over 800,000 applications available for smartphones, depending on the operating system (Global mobile 2013). Obviously, there are fewer applications that have been developed strictly or primarily for law enforcement personnel. Several URLs identify various smartphone applications for policing and/or private investigators: www.policeone.com/police-iphone-apps/ lists 12 apps; www.policeipho neapps.com/ lists 21 apps; and www.appsforinvestigators.com/ lists 9. Author Tim Dees (trainer and former law enforcement officer) and editor Doug Wyllie are frequent writers on technology applied to policing for PoliceOne.com and they have reviewed several smartphone apps for law enforcement personnel (see: Dees 2013, 2011; Wyllie 2014, 2013; PoliceOne.Com 2014). Others also have identified worthwhile apps for policing (Roberts 2013; Basich 2013; Scullin 2012; Pogue 2012).

Emerging applications include devices to attach to smartphones to utilize their computing and connectivity capabilities in order to analyze substances, drugs, and DNA. There are several smartphone breathalyzers (Breathometer Breeze, Alcohoot, BACtrack Mobile, BACtrack Vio) on the market for personal use, but we are not aware that any have such proven technology as to be admissible in court. There is also interest in developing a portable (possibly a smartphone app) breathalyzer device for the detection of marijuana. Cannabix Technologies in July 2015 was reportedly testing a prototype device that can accurately detect the presence of tetrahydrocannabinol (THC) in a person's system. The device can detect the presence of THC but not a quantitative measure (Heisler 2015). In August 2015, the Cannabix company of Canada entered into an agreement with Yost Research Group at the University of Florida to develop devices that can measure marijuana levels within an individual; "Our objective is to develop a handheld breathalyzer that will provide precise medical grade and court accepted results at the roadside" (Cannabix 2015: para. 3).

CAMERAS AND VIDEO

While much of the investigative process in law enforcement involves documenting the scene of a crime or incident after it has occurred, it is possible with today's technology to begin the investigative and documentation process prior to, and while, the incident is unfolding. In the past, piecing together the incident after it had occurred would entail interviewing victims, witnesses, and others that were involved in the incident, possibly including the involved officer or officers. The resulting documentation was subjected to the imperfections of memory; the bias, real or alleged, of the witnesses; and purposeful misleading testimony. As noted by Mackey and Courtney (in Chapter 3), video camera technology is providing the means to record an incident as it happens, allowing patrol officers to capture a plethora of data concerning the incident – when it works (see Turowski's discussion concerning cameras and reliability, in Chapter 7).

However, attempts to obtain real-time recordings of a crime are not new. In the late nineteenth and early twentieth centuries, some police departments photographed the eyes of murder victims hoping to find an image of the murderer recorded on the retinas. The most notorious case where this was done involved Scotland Yard's investigation into a murder attributed to Jack the Ripper (Evans 1993). This crime scene technique was based upon several experiments. One such experiment involved a rabbit, held in a stationary position, and looking at a known scene. The rabbit was decapitated immediately after, had its eyeballs removed and cut open; then the retina was placed in a chemical bath. Reportedly, an image of the last scene that was viewed by the rabbit developed on the retina (Wald 1953; in Evans 1993). Obviously, the practice of photographing a victim's eyes for this purpose is not used today in an attempt to gain a recording of an incident in progress.

Technology has provided the ability for police officers to record video and audio from an in-car system and from a body-worn camera. This ability, while beneficial in many ways, also presents a problem. As Turowski notes in Chapter 7, most in-car video systems are triggered, or placed in record mode, by activating the emergency lights (Griffith 2015, May); thus, if an officer makes a traffic stop, the in-car system is triggered and recording begins. If the traffic stop turns into a foot pursuit, the incident will quickly move out of the recording area of the car. In this case, the officer would have to activate the body-worn camera, since most in use today do not trigger automatically. However, some systems are becoming integrated. Digital Ally is marketing a system that automatically triggers the body-worn camera when the in-car camera is triggered. Conversely, the in-car camera can be triggered if the body-worn camera becomes active. Further, this integrated system has the ability to trigger all body-worn cameras (of a particular model) within a certain range of the car involved (Griffith 2015, June). Additionally, one system by Digital Ally can tag the body-worn camera data, and the cruiser camera data as being related, which makes data retrieval much easier (PoliceOne.Com 2014).

In-car cameras and body-worn cameras are not the only recording devices that can be used by police officers. Phazzer® Electronics is marketing a product they call the RailCam[tm]. This device is a recording camera that is made to mount on top of the Enforcer®, one of the conductive energy weapons manufactured by Phazzer® Electronics. The camera is removable and can also be used on a pistol or rifle that is equipped with the proper mounting system. The camera has 8 GB of storage capacity, approximately 90 minutes of recording time. Captured data is transferred via a USB connection to a computer or storage device (Law and Order Staff 2014, December), however questions will remain regarding transferability and interface with other systems.

A further consideration is the ability of any of these systems to store and retrieve the data once collected. An advertisement in the January 1, 1990, issue of *InfoWorld* magazine showed a 20-MB hard disk drive for the price of $239.00 (Modern Business Systems 1990: 66). At the present time, it is possible to purchase a 16-GB thumb drive for about $10.00. In other words, the thumb drive can hold 800 times more data than the 1990 hard disk drive at about four percent of the cost. It is this dramatic increase in data storage capacity that has made the efficient use of police camera systems possible.

When data are captured by a camera, they are stored on some type of computer media. In the case of many body-worn cameras, the captured data are stored on flash memory within the camera unit (Meyer n.d.). When the memory reaches capacity, the data must be moved to another storage device and the memory cleared for further recording. The camera is then ready to store additional information. In an analysis from the City of San Antonio (TX), it was estimated that an officer will generate about 3 hours of video and that the storage requirements to store that video data will be about 2.7 GB (Kozlowski 2015, June). Assume that a small police department has ten officers, and each officer generates 2.7 GB of data per day. In a year, the total space to store the video would be 9,855 GB or more that 9.8 terabytes (TB) of storage space. Without the ability to store and retrieve the information, the recording process would be of little value.

While the cost of computer storage has fallen dramatically, as shown above, and while it will most likely continue to drop, it is still relatively expensive to purchase the hardware to store and manage that much data. The data storage aspect will most probably be the greatest expense of a body-worn (or any) camera system (Griffith 2015, June). Further, as more video is captured, the need to expand computer storage capabilities will always be a possibility. Also keep in mind that video captured by in-car video systems will also need to be stored. For these reasons, some departments may consider cloud storage solutions. The cloud can be defined as "a web-based network of servers used to store and access data and software through the Internet" (Hardy 2015: 22). In such a situation, the video data is transferred to remote, web-based storage devices. An additional benefit is that the data can be searched and organized using the data management software provided by the cloud storage provider (Hardy 2015).

CRIME SCENE-RELATED TECHNOLOGIES

In addition to vehicular technologies, the use of vicinity surveillance cameras is becoming more valuable in crime identification and investigation since it can provide photographic/visual evidence of subjects who were in the area of an incident. As of July 2015, the city of Corpus Christi (TX) was planning a citywide camera interoperability project which will be able to track suspects remotely, in real time, through surveillance cameras being monitored from police headquarters (Alvarado 2015). The monitoring technology is similar to the Philadelphia Police Department's Real-Time Crime Center (RTCC) that went operational in 2012. The RTCC has "access to nearly 2,000 surveillance camera feeds and automated license plate scanners" (Reyes 2013: para. 1). Similar RTCCs are now operational in New York (NY), Houston (TX), St. Louis (MO), Albuquerque (NM), Ogden (UT), Memphis (TN), Rochester (NY),

Fresno (CA), and Daytona Beach (FL), to name a few. Capabilities of RTCCs vary but capabilities that enhance investigations include surveillance camera recordings, data mining of multiple databases, crime analysis, link analysis, shot-spotter integration, license plate recognition, etc.

RTCCs have the potential of providing significant amounts of timely information for patrol and investigative personnel; such centers may actually record the crime while in progress, prior to any officers ever being present. The technology can then be used to provide responding officers with information that may assist in locating and apprehending offenders more quickly. Investigators can be provided relevant details of the incident along with crime analysis and any information about known suspects.

The actual recording of a crime scene for investigation and forensic analysis has taken major leaps forward in the digital age. Still images/photos are still used, but today they can be digital; and video recordings are often used as well. The most recent technology available for recording crime scenes is "panoramic imaging technology," sometimes referred to a "3-D laser scanning." "3D laser technology is enabling forensic scientists to capture accurate representations of crime scenes and then virtually reconstruct those scenes to help them better understand the environment and the events that took place" (Grahl 2013: para. 2). Such technology allows investigators to return to the crime scene multiple times because of the data and images stored electronically. Items not originally deemed as evidence can later be identified as such and analyzed accordingly. The results of the scan can also be displayed in court as a video recording of the scene (Wangler 2015).

Once the crime scene has been documented, evidence identification, labeling, collection, and storage must be assured. Galvin reminds us that managing evidence is critical; that for some agencies it is overwhelming because of insufficient training, low priority, or rotating personnel; other agencies are superb at it through automation (Galvin 2013).

Automated evidence management systems are needed and usually are of two types: (a) integrated into an agency's record management system (RMS) or (b) standalone systems. Both systems can benefit the agency's management of evidence and both have various benefits. Some departments may not want to integrate their evidence management software into the RMS because of cost, complexity, and/or data entry requirements. As software development improves in this arena, it will become easier to integrate standalone systems into record management systems to allow real-time analysis of evidentiary items that may be related to other cases (Galvin 2013).

Another type of scanner, one that takes a close-up look at an object, can be used to capture a digital, high-resolution, full color, 3-dimentional image of an object. Once digitized, the image can be rotated, and viewed from different angles, "as if you were actually holding it in your hand" (DeLaurentis 2009: 37). This technology has the potential to impact forensic science in many ways. Once captured digitally, the image can be transmitted to those authorized to view it in very little time. Also, since "many physical samples are temporary or fragile in nature" and at the same time, they contain "precious information that isn't easily shared through physical means," this technology makes it possible to preserve evidence forever and store it digitally without taking up precious physical storage space (DeLaurentis 2009: 40). An additional benefit of the digital image capture of a physical item is that the image can then be used to reproduce the item with a 3-D printer.

Impressions in snow, powder, or other soft materials, footprints, and tool marks lend themselves to this type of data capture as a supplement to the normal evidence collection process. Another benefit of 3-D scanning involves the actual item or tool that left the impression. It can also be scanned and the image of the impression can be compared, digitally, to the suspected item.

Laboratory Equipment/Technique Advances

DNA

Obviously, one of the most critical advancements in crime laboratory analysis during the last two decades has been the improvement in DNA analysis. Today, unknown tissue or body fluid samples found at a crime scene can be matched against a known sample through analysis of deoxyribonucleic acid (DNA). The process is referred to DNA profiling or genetic fingerprinting. Samples of known offenders are maintained in the national database known as CODIS (Combined DNA Index System). Of course, other known samples can be obtained in local investigations from persons of interest, family members, or other known persons. DNA findings have been used to solve cold cases and even to exonerate convicted persons; reports of such incidents are common.

DNA analysis known as touch DNA has been available for about 5 years (Ritter 2008; Minor 2013). It involves using "small samples of

DNA from evidence that has been handled by suspects. Items such as vehicle steering wheels, gun grips, door handles, and victim's clothing have provided valuable evidence linking offenders to a victim or crime scene" (Weiss 2015: para. 1). Unfortunately, touch DNA analysis has been so successful in some jurisdictions that the lab has had to restrict it to violent crimes only, and may be caused by a fear of resource overload (Augenstein 2015).

Emerging in the field of DNA analysis is the production of a DNA profile in the form of a photo or descriptive composite when no matches to known specimens occur; this is known as DNA phenotyping. This is a prediction of certain physical characteristics (e.g. eye, skin and hair color; and face shape) based on the DNA profile. (Maybe you have heard of obtaining your ancestry based on a DNA sample.) If an investigation is stymied, but there is a DNA sample that can be analyzed, an agency could consider pursuing this technique (Dees 2015).

Another innovation, regarding DNA analysis, is the recording of a DNA profile at the time of booking with a system known as Rapid DNA Analysis. Such technology can produce a profile in about 90 minutes. The Rapid DNA technology is currently in use in a number of "states, as well as China, Russia, Australia, and countries in Africa and Europe" (Bauer 2014: para. 3). Other agencies are awaiting validation studies before investing in the expensive equipment. Garvey (2015) has noted that no Rapid DNA instrument has received the approval required for uploading or comparing profiles with CODIS.

Bacteria Analysis

According to Weiss, the next phase of forensic development in the DNA arena will be bacterial fingerprinting. Based on several research studies to date that involved finger and genital bacteria matching, she thinks that this type of forensic analysis will play a major role in the future investigation of cases involving cellphones and sexual assaults (Weiss 2015). Another study involved computer keyboards that were swabbed for bacteria, analyzed, and matched to users with a very high rate of accuracy (Loria 2014). It is not far-fetched to believe that such analyses will be common one day for purposes of criminal investigations.

Substance Identification and Fingerprints

Intelligent Fingerprinting, which is currently being developed and tested in the United Kingdom, is different from the current technologies that are used to develop and lift latent fingerprints. While this new technology can accomplish the traditional latent fingerprint development, it can also provide some information about the lifestyle of the person who left the print by analyzing substances in the residue that forms the print. This lifestyle information can involve such things as whether or not the owner of the fingerprint abuses drugs or uses nicotine.

When a person leaves a fingerprint on a surface, secretions from the eccrine, or sweat glands, are left behind with the fingerprint. These secretions, commonly called sweat, "come directly from the pores in the friction ridge skin" (Mayo 2012: 21). In addition to biological material such as creatinine and amino acids, the secretions may also contain metabolites, which are chemicals produced by the body's normal metabolic processes. Since these metabolites result from specific substances that were metabolized by the body, identifying the metabolites will identify the original substances. An example given by Mayo is the metabolite, cotinine. This substance is the metabolite of nicotine and will be found in the person's urine, serum, and sweat. Detecting this substance in the sweat deposited with the fingerprint will establish nicotine use by the owner of the print (Mayo 2012).

The company that developed this technology is called Intelligent Fingerprinting, Ltd. and had its origin at the University of East Anglia in the United Kingdom. Metabolite identification is accomplished with the use of high-sensitivity reagents. Each reagent, which is specific to a particular metabolite, is a combination of either gold or iron, which is bound to antibodies by certain "proteins and linker molecules" (Mayo 2012: 21). These small particles, called nanoparticles, will then bind to the specific metabolic antigens in the fingerprint. To date, reagents have been developed to identify cocaine metabolite, methadone metabolite, Morphine, and Tetrahydrocannabinol. Morphine is the metabolite of heroin and Tetrahydrocannabinol is the main active substance in the cannabis plant.

Magnification of the developed fingerprint will show that the heaviest concentration of the metabolite is at the site of each pore on the friction ridges and spreads along the ridge from there. This offers evidence that the metabolite did in fact originate with the excretions from the pores, and is not from a contaminating source or direct contact with another subject. Additionally, fingerprints developed with the Intelligent Fingerprint system can be magnified to show clear details of the ridge shapes, pore structure, and fine ridge detail. The company believes that this may lead to "the development of improved, higher match probability when comparing fingerprints" (Mayo 2012: 22).

Limitations, Precautions, and Policy Implications

In this section, we review some of the limitations, precautions, and policy implications of selected technologies. It is not a comprehensive review of all investigation-related technologies, but it is hoped that the issues will assist in understanding the complexities and potential problems if technologies are implemented without their consideration. The use of technology in policing and criminal investigations is constantly evolving, but its potential abuse complicates its acceptance by the general public. As new devices emerge, sometimes there is a major gap in the broad use of the technology and the protection of perceived individual rights and liberties. The National Security Agency has the ability to intercept phone calls and has done so, but the public sentiment doesn't totally support massive collection of domestic phone call information or data-mining of that data. Unmanned aircraft systems (UAS; aka, drones) are being deployed or tested by hundreds of law enforcement agencies in the United States, but communities are enacting ordinances restricting their use; states are passing statutes, and the Federal Aviation Administration issued its first regulations in late June 2016.

The overall use of technology in policing is highly dependent on available resources. The 2013 Law Enforcement Management and Administrative Statistics (LEMAS) survey of over 2,000 local police departments of all sizes, indicated the following (Reaves 2015: 1–3)

- The percentage of local police departments that authorized their officers to use conducted energy weapons such as Tasers increased... to 81% in 2013.
- The percentage of local police departments that required officers to wear protective armor at all times increased... to 71% in 2013.
- From 2007 to 2013, the percentage of local police departments using in-car video cameras increased... to 68%.

- About a third (32%) of local police departments used body-worn cameras in 2013.
- About one in six local police departments used automated vehicle license plate readers in 2013, including a majority of those serving a population of 25,000 or more.
- More than 90% of local police departments serving 25,000 or more residents provided patrol officers with in-field computerized access to vehicle records, driving records, and outstanding warrants.
- Among local police departments serving 10,000 or more residents, more than 90% had their own website and more than 80% used social media.
- About 60% of local police departments provided crime statistics to citizens electronically, including more than 90% of those serving 25,000 or more residents.
- By 2013, a majority of the departments in each population category were using in-car cameras. Overall, 68% (about 8,400) of all departments used in-car cameras in 2013.

When one closely analyzes the LEMAS data, a few disturbing findings emerge: (a) video technology (in-car and body-worn cameras) is not as common as many believe, (b) the availability of conducted energy weapons is not universal, and (c) other than the variable of population size served, no analysis is made regarding region of country, budgetary variables, external grant funding, community racial diversity, crime rates, etc.; each of which deserves far greater examination moving forward.

Cameras and Surveillance

After several high-profile incidents involving police officers that resulted in the deaths of subjects during the years of 2014 and 2015, the public, the president, Congress, and many state officials called for increased use of body-worn cameras for officers. In May of 2015, the U.S. Justice Department announced the availability of $20 million in funding for police body cameras; the funds are the first of a $75 million, 3-year initiative to expand their use in policing. Based on the 2013 LEMAS data, the funding should increase the percentage of departments using such technology, see Table 6.1.

As Turowski notes in Chapter 7, there are several limitations and concerns such as cost considerations, file storage, privacy rights, public record access issues related to body cameras (Dees 2014; White 2014), and

Table 6.1   Use of selected video technologies by local police departments, by size of population, 2013

Population served	Types used by patrol officer				Other types		
	Any type	In-car video camera	Body-worn camera	Weapon-attached camera	Cameras for surveillance of public areas	License plate readers	Unmanned aerial drones
All sizes	76%	68%	32%	6%	49%	17%	–
1,000,000 or more	71	57	21	14	86	93	7%
500,000–999,999	80	73	30	7	87	77	3
250,000–499,999	70	63	20	9	87	87	2
100,000–249,999	75	70	19	10	76	77	1
50,000–99,999	70	63	26	11	68	55	0
25,000–49,999	79	76	22	9	67	50	0
10,000–24,999	75	71	26	9	62	24	0
2,500–9,999	80	71	34	8	51	10	0
2,499 or fewer	72	64	35	3	35	6	0

Source: Reaves 2015, Law Enforcement Management and Administrative Statistics (LEMAS) Survey, 2013, Table 3

legislative and administrative guidelines have yet to properly address these matters across the United States.

Privacy concerns are emerging as the primary issue surrounding all forms of surveillance; it will undoubtedly be several years before courts rule on the privacy rights associated with body cameras, drones, real-time surveillance systems, and automated license plate scanners (Dixon 2015). Complicating these issues are the layers of governmental regulations and legislation that impact such rulings. Some states have "privacy" clauses in their constitutions and other states have certain restrictions in legislative enactments; federal laws and regulations may be limited to federal buildings and property (unless rulings of the U.S. Supreme Court apply to the states).

As this chapter was being written, the Department of Justice issued new policies on the use of cell-site simulators (cell phone tracking systems – aka, Stingray, Kingfish, or Hailstorm). The new Department rules apply to all Department agencies to "enhance transparency and accountability, improve training and supervision, establish a higher and more consistent legal standard and increase privacy protections in relation to law enforcement's use of this critical technology" (Department of Justice, September 3, 2015a, para. 1). A seven-page policy guidance has been issued by the Department which outlines (a) the need for a search warrant to use such technology, (b) what can and cannot be obtained, (c) management controls, and (d) exceptions (Department of Justice Policy Guidelines 2015b). It should be noted that the new guidelines are just that, guidelines; and they do not apply to other federal or state or local agencies.

Summary

Technological advances in policing are evolving rapidly. Their use in every-day policing and investigation is emerging piecemeal throughout the United States in a complex and litigious environment. Lagging behind these technologies are the legislative and administrative guidelines, best practices, and restrictions. Incidents in one part of the country that abuse these technologies may adversely affect their deployment in other areas of the nation. Professional groups have developed recommendations and guidelines for the use of many of these technologies, and it is highly recommended that agencies conduct proper research and seek legal advice prior to utilization of many of the technologies presented in this chapter. Society runs the risk of restricting the use of some of these technologies by law enforcement agencies when the same restrictions are NOT applied to the private sector – thus allowing the law-breaking element of society to gain a technological advantage over law enforcement personnel and activities.

REFERENCES

Alvarado, B. (2015, July 17). Corpus Christi, Texas, PD to deploy citywide camera interoperability project. *Corpus Christi Caller-Times*, Texas. Reprinted in Government Technology. Available at: http://www.govtech.com/dc/arti cles/Corpus-Christi-Texas-PD-to-Deploy-Citywide-Camera-Interoperability-Project.htm.

Augenstein, S. (2015, July 7). Too much touch DNA evidence overwhelms a Texas county crime lab. *Forensic Magazine*. Available at: http://www.forensi cmag.com/articles/2015/07/too-much-touch-dna-evidence-overwhelms-texas-county-crime-lab.

Basich, M. (2013, March 25). 10 great LE mobile apps. *Police*. Available at: http://www.policemag.com/channel/technology/articles/2013/03/10-great-le-mobile-apps.aspx.

Bauer, S. (2014, November 20). The FBI is very excited about this machine that can scan your DNA in 90 minutes. Available at: http://www.motherjones.com/politics/2014/11/rapid-dna-profiles-database-fbi-police.

Cannabix Technologies. (2015, August 11). Cannabix technologies partners with University of Florida to develop marijuana breath test devices. *News Release*. Available at: http://www.cannabixtechnologies.com/news-releases.html.

Dees, T. (2011, June 20). *3 great police iPhone apps*. *PoliceOne.com*. Retrieved from http://www.policeone.com/police-products/investigation/Investigative-Software/articles/3834049-3-great-police-iPhoneapps/.

Dees, T. (2013, December 10). 4 helpful police smartphone apps for android. *PoliceOne.com*. Available at: http://www.policeone.com/police-products/police-technology/articles/6645023-4-helpful-police-smartphone-apps-for-Android/.

Dees, T. (2014, December 3). Why Obama's bodycam initiative won't work. *PoliceOne.com*. Available at: http://www.policeone.com/police-products/body-cameras/articles/7921687-Why-Obamas-bodycam-initiative-wont-work/.

Dees, T. (2015, January 27). *A new way DNA tech can help you ID your unknown suspect*. PoliceOne.com. Retrieved from http://www.policeone.com/investiga tions/articles/8193116-A-new-way-DNA-tech-canhelp-you-ID-your-unknown-suspect/.

DeLaurentis, P. (2009, February-March). 3D Scanning: A new tool for cracking tough cases. *Forensic Magazine*, *61*(1), 37–40.

Department of Justice. (2015a, September 3). Justice department announces enhanced policy for use of cell-site simulators. *Press Release*. Available at:

http://www.justice.gov/opa/pr/justice-department-announces-enhanced-policy-use-cell-site-simulators.

Department of Justice. (2015b, September 3). Policy guidelines: Use of cell-site simulator technology. Available at: http://www.justice.gov/opa/file/767321/download.

Dixon, M. (2015, February 12). Florida's police body camera bill runs into privacy concerns. *Naples Daily News.* Available at: http://www.govtech.com/products/Floridas-Police-Body-Camera-Bill-Runs-Into-Privacy-Concerns.html.

Evans, A. B. (1993). Optograms and fiction: Photo in a dead man's eye. *Science Fiction Studies, 20*(3), 341–361. Available at: http://works.bepress.com/arthur_evans/12/.

Galvin, B. (2013, February 22). Electronic evidence management. Available at: http://www.policemag.com/channel/technology/articles/2013/02/electronic-evidence-management.aspx.

Garvey, M. (2015, June 18). Rapid DNA analysis: What is it, and should you be using it? *Law Officer.* Available at: http://www.lawofficer.com/articles/2015/06/rapid-dna-analysis.html.

Global mobile statistics (2013 Section E). *Mobile apps, app stores, pricing and failure rates mobiThinking – 2013, May 26.* Retrieved from http://mobiforge.com/research-analysis/global-mobile-statistics-2013-section-e-mobile-apps-app-stores-pricing-and-failure-rates#lotsofapps.

Grahl, C. (2013). Investigating crime scenes using 3D laser technology. [Podcast] Available at: http://hxgnnews.com/investigating-crime-scenes-using-3d-laser-technology/.

Griffith, D. (2015, May). Kings of the road. *Police, 39*(5), 48–51.

Griffith, D. (2015, June). What to look for in body cameras and storage solutions. *Special Report: Body-Worn Cameras, Police, 39*(6), 22–23.

Hardy, M. (2015, August). Why take public safety data into the cloud?. *Police, 39*(8), 22–24.

Heisler, Y. (2015, July 17). Marijuana breathalyzer being developed to keep potheads off the road. *BGR Media.* Available at: http://bgr.com/2015/07/17/marijuana-breathalyzer-development-thc-levels/.

Kozlowski, J. (2015, June). A few things you might want to think about on cloud storage. *Law Enforcement Technology, 43*(6), 8–11.

Law and Order Staff. (2014, December). Phazzer HD DVR Railcam. *Law and Order, 62*(12), 24–29.

Loria, K. (2014, March 20). *How To Identify Where Someone's Been — Without A Fingerprint Or Human DNA.* Business Insider. Retrieved from http://www.businessinsider.com/skin-bacteria-identifies-you-2014-3#ixzz3iRjre9re.

Mayo, K. (2012, March-April). Beyond identification. *Evidence Technology Magazine, 10*(2), 20–25.

Meyer, G. (n.d.). Drafting your agency's body-worn camera policy. *Special Report: Body-Worn Cameras, Police.*

Minor, J. (2013, April 12). Touch DNA: From the Crime Scene to the Crime Laboratory. *Forensic Magazine.* Retrieved from http://www.forensicmag. com/articles/2013/04/touch-dna-crime-scene-crime-laboratory.

Modern Business Systems. (1990, January 1). *InfoWorld, 12*(1), 66. Available at: https://books.google.com/books?id=gzAEAAAAMBAJ%26pg=PA66% 26lpg=PA66%26dq=seagate%B20mg%B1drive%26source=bl%26ots= AphHqgxVVy%26sig=DaHB9q3qNivgO-zJTDSBsjcN31U%26hl=en%26sa=X %26ved=0CCYQ6AEwBGoVChMIkrjnvPHqxwIVA5UeCh1l5Qmz#v=one page%26q=seagate%2020mg%20drive%26f=false.

Pogue, D. (2012, September 5). Smartphone? Presto! 2-Way Radio. *NYTimes. com.* Available at: http://www.nytimes.com/2012/09/06/technology/per sonaltech/zello-heytell-and-voxer-make-your-smartphone-a-walkie-talkie-david-pogue.html?pagewanted=all&_r=0.

PoliceOne.Com (2014). Living the future of in-car video with Digital Ally. Available at: http://www.policeone.com/police-products/vehicle-equip ment/in-car-video/articles/7004975-Living-the-future-of-in-car-video-with-Digital-Ally/.

Reaves, B. A. (2015, July). Local police departments, 2013: Equipment and tech-nology. NCJ 248767. Available at: http://www.bjs.gov/index.cfm?ty=pbdetai l&iid=5321.

Reyes, J. (2013, February 20). Real Time Crime Center: 1 year after launch, 24-hour support center will move to Delaware Valley Intelligence Center this spring. *Technically Philly.* Available at: http://technical.ly/philly/2013/02/ 20/real-time-crime-center-1-year-after-launch-24-hour-support-center-will-move-to-delaware-valley-intelligence-center-this-spring/.

Ritter, N. (2008). DNA Solves Property Crimes (But Are We Ready for That?). *NIJ Journal* (261). https://www.ncjrs.gov/pdffiles1/nij/224084.pdf.

Roberts, J. (2013). 33 police apps for law enforcement officers & future crime fighters. Bloomington, MN: Rasmussen College. Available at: http://www. rasmussen.edu/degrees/justice-studies/blog/police-apps-law-enforcement-officers-criminal-justice-students/.

Scullin, S. (2012, June 15). 20 ways to use your smartphone. *Officer.com.* Available at: http://www.officer.com/article/10719373/20-ways-to-use-your-smartphone.

Wald, G. (1953). Eye and camera. *Scientific American Reader*, 555–568 in Evans, A. B. (1993). Optograms and fiction: Photo in a dead man's eye. *Science Fiction Studies, 20*(3), 341–361. Available at: from http://works.bepress.com/ arthur_evans/12/.

Wangler, B. (2015, June 11). 2015 Innovation awards – faro crime scene scanner. Larimer County, CO. Available at: https://www.youtube.com/watch?v= 3sBPTt1DZ0w.

Weiss, D. (2015, January 26). LE investigation tools expand beyond DNA to bacteria. American Military University. Available at: http://inpublicsafety.com/2015/01/law-enforcement-investigation-tools-expand-beyond-dna-to-bacteria/.

White, M. (2014). *Police officer body-worn cameras, assessing the evidence.* Washington, DC: Department of Justice. Available at: https://www.ojpdiagnosticcenter.org/sites/default/files/spotlight/download/Police%20Officer%20Body-Worn%20Cameras.pdf.

Wyllie, D. (2013). *IACP 2013: Motorola puts P25 LMR signal into your LTE-enabled smartphone.* PoliceOne.com. 2013, October 21. Retrieved from http://www.policeone.com/policeproducts/communications/articles/6537063-IACP-2013-Motorola-puts-P25-LMR-signal-into-your-LTE-enabledsmartphone/.

Wyllie, D. (2014). *Harris puts P25 PTT on smartphones, tablets, and other devices.* PoliceOne.com. 2014, February 11. Retrieved from http://www.policeone.com/policeproducts/communications/articles/6852388-Harris-puts-P25-PTT-on-smartphones-tablets-and-other-devices/.

James A. Conser is Professor Emeritus at Youngstown State University (Ohio), Adjunct Professor at the University of Mount Union and currently the Criminal Justice Internship Coordinator in the Sociology and Criminal Justice Department. He previously served as the Deputy Director of the Ohio Peace Officer Training Commission (OPOTC) from January of 1999 through December of 2002. Jim holds a PhD in Higher Education Administration and a MSc in Criminal Justice. Jim began his career as a police officer in Arlington County, Virginia. He is a Certified Protection Professional through ASIS International. He is coauthor of *Law Enforcement in the United States* (2013) and *Police Personnel Systems* (1983). He is a lifetime member of the Society of Police Futurists International (PFI) and was national secretary for 9 years. He is also a lifetime member of the Academy of Criminal Justice Sciences, a member of the Ohio Crime Prevention Association, and the Ohio Criminal Justice Education Association.

Louis P. Carsone is the Director of Public Safety for the City of Hubbard, Ohio, USA. He is a retired Police Officer of the City after 31 years of full-time service, having served as a Patrol Sergeant and Police Chief. He holds a bachelor's degree in Law Enforcement Administration and a Master of Science degree in Criminal Justice, both from the Youngstown State University. He has authored several articles on the topic of "law enforcement's use of computers" and has instructed courses on police use of computer technology. He is currently certified as a Basic Police Academy Instructor in Ohio, instructing for several local Police Academies.

CHAPTER 7

Technology Limitations in Policing (The Reality is . . .)

Andrew Turowski

Abstract This chapter will discuss some of the most common issues and concerns associated with some of the modern technologies that are currently available to law enforcement. It will make use of the areas previously discussed, but provide for a real world, contextual position. It will consider body-worn cameras and electronic control devices, to social media, drones, and records management technology; each has its own set of issues that are being brought to light in an effort to allow law enforcement agencies to better implement these technologies.

Keywords Body camera · Drone · Limitations · Records management · In-car camera · Reality

Introduction

Not long ago, an officer who had worked some 50 years in law enforcement, who was now in his seventies, decided to call it a career and retire. On occasion, that officer would talk about how things "use to be." He would talk of times where the police were well respected

---

A. Turowski (✉)
Chief of Police, Louisville Police Department, Louisville, Ohio, USA
e-mail: turowsan@mountunion.edu or aturowsk@kent.edu

A. Bain (ed.), *Law Enforcement and Technology*,
DOI 10.1057/978-1-137-57915-7_7

and relied very little on technology. It's funny how the climate and social context can change.

One of his most frequent stories was the account of how he would collect money from the parking meters in the downtown area during the midnight shift. He said that when an officer was out of the patrol car, collecting money, they would know if there was a call for service because the dispatcher would activate a series of small red lights that hung in various locations in the downtown area. At that point the officer would know to return to his patrol car and communicate with the dispatcher via a VHF (very high frequency), two-way radio. Today, in that same Ohio suburban police department, officers carry an 800-megahertz portable radio on their hip that is interoperable to the point that it can communicate with virtually every police and fire department in the county as well as hospitals, health departments, public transportation organizations, and emergency management agencies. Times have certainly changed.

As noted in previous chapters in this text, advancements in technology have, without question, improved many aspects of law enforcement. From mobile data terminals and shared databases (discussed by Mackey and Courtney in Chapter 3), to electronic control devices and body-worn cameras (see Conser and Carsone, Chapter 6), technology has made policing safer, more efficient and more effective. However, for as much as we have benefited from modern technology, technology in police work should be viewed with a critical mind and cautious optimism. Our favorite police television shows such as CSI and Criminal Minds would lead one to believe that the technology that exists in law enforcement not only has limitless capabilities, but also never fails. The reality is that nothing could be further from the truth.

This chapter will discuss a number of modern technologies related to twenty-first century law enforcement as well as considerations and concerns associated with each one. As Mackey and Courtney have stated, there is a large list of technologies that are available and an even larger list of companies that provide different versions of those technologies. Policeone.com notes more than thirty providers of body-worn camera systems to choose from alone. In the absence of a preferred provider list (provided by an objective reviewer), each agency is left to determine which provider is best for them. This process alone can be a daunting task. Blind faith and the purchase of technology should never go hand-in-hand. Promises made in the sales meeting won't always come to fruition. Before an agency considers the use of any new technology, careful consideration has to be given to what the agency is trying to accomplish, if the technology is compatible with existing operations and budget limitations and if the provider is a viable partner in the endeavor. Not carefully considering these issues could prove a precursor to future failure.

This discussion will primarily focus on contemporary technologies that pose the need for careful consideration prior to implementation in local and state law enforcement agencies. Specifically, it will consider body-worn cameras, electronic control devices, social media, drone technology and digital records management.

Body-Worn Cameras (BWC)

As Conser and Carsone have correctly noted, body-worn cameras have been at the forefront of policing in recent years, and never-more-so than following the recent, and numerous, examples of unarmed citizens being killed by police officers. Thus, providing us with good reason to see the body-worn camera as a technology at the forefront for law enforcement, but also for the public and politicians as well.

There have been, unfortunately, a number of public incidents in the past several years that challenge, if not impugn, the integrity of law enforcement in the minds of many people. As Bain noted in Chapter 4, as with most professions, it only takes a few "bad ones" to bring a shadow of doubt over everyone. For example, Weitzer and Tuch (2005: 282) noted that

> If exposure to media reports on one incident of abuse lowers public approval of the police, we might predict that cumulative exposure to media coverage of separate instances of police misconduct will have an even stronger effect on citizens' opinions of the police.

This position was later confirmed in a report from the NIJ (2014) which suggested that frequent exposure to media reports of police abuse or corruption is a strong predictor of perceptions of misconduct and supports the belief that it is common. With the recent, seemingly non-stop national news coverage of alleged police misconduct in Ferguson (MO), Cleveland (OH), North Charleston (SC), Baton Rouge (LO), and a number of other cities, the impact of these incidents by a few officers has negatively affected the image of police everywhere. Indeed, with the rise in social media, where once these shooting may have seemed more isolated and rare occurrences, they now dominate hours of news media reporting and internet space.

Many, to include the U.S. Attorney General, see body-worn cameras as the answer to the problem of questionable police conduct and activity. In May of 2015, when announcing the availability of Department of Justice funds to purchase body-worn cameras, Attorney General Loretta Lynch said, "Body-worn cameras hold tremendous promise for enhancing transparency, promoting accountability and advancing public safety for law enforcement officers and the communities they serve" (Berman 2015: para 5). And, while many are likely to agree that these devices can be enormously beneficial, if the application and use is to be successful, there are other issues to consider before an agency delves into this technology.

The first issue, but likely the simplest issue to address in the current environment, is cost. In most local and state law enforcement organizations, there is only so much money to go around and there are, almost certainly, competing interests for that money. While there may be grants available to help pay for the upfront expense, there are ongoing costs to be considered related to body-worn cameras. Some of these costs include repair, replacement, additional information technology requirements, and additional work related to processing of evidence and public records requests. All of these come at an expense to the department, the governmental body, and ultimately the taxpayer. The person responsible for resource development or funding within the agency should ensure new funding streams to facilitate the long term use of this technology, or risk reductions, or cuts elsewhere in the agency's budget. Having a technology intended to increase accountability that the agency does not or cannot maintain, could be worse than not having the technology at all. As body-worn cameras become a priority, something else may fall further down the list of importance such as vehicles, weapons, or even training, all important components of police operations. Consorted efforts must be undertaken to inform the officials who make the funding decisions for the agency about the importance of this technology as well as the requirement for ongoing funding to maintain a body-worn camera program.

Another consideration surrounds the issue of privacy. Body-worn cameras go where the officer goes, and often officers have access to some of the most private areas of an individual's life, an issue raised by

Conser and Carsone earlier in this text. Until laws related to public records are updated to reflect this type of technology, the public may have the opportunity to see everything that the officer sees, regardless of how compromising or inappropriate. Currently, in the State of Ohio, absent very limited circumstances, body-worn camera footage, much like in-car camera footage, becomes public record upon the adjudication of a criminal case, if not sooner in a circumstance where there are no criminal allegations. While good common sense should prevail, agencies should be careful to implement policies that are not only consistent with public record law, but that also take into account the privacy rights of those they serve. Some agencies have mandated in policy that the officers inform the party that they are being recorded, which does address some of the privacy concerns. However, most officers will tell you that telling someone that they are being recorded or the thought of making an official record can cause a great deal of reluctance on the part of a victim or witness to cooperate. Privacy concerns with body-worn cameras are, as with most privacy issues, a constant but necessary balancing act.

Finally, and maybe most important, body-worn cameras cannot be viewed as the solution to all of our problems. There is little doubt that this type of technology will improve accountability of officers, but, as with any technology, sometimes it will fail. Sometimes they will not record what needs to be recorded.

As previously stated, an in-car video system is meant to capture the activity around and inside of a police vehicle. A body-worn camera system is "specifically designed to capture a single officer's point of view..." (Griffith 2015). Whilst this phrase may seem to be very straightforward and not need much clarification, it is anything but that. For example, to capture an officer's point of view, the camera would need to see what the officer is seeing. That's easily stated, but more difficult to accomplish. Today's technology has created a variety of camera systems that can be worn in various locations on the body; on the chest, on the shoulder, or a head-mounted unit. Each of these presents a different view. Further, each presents a chance that part of the view of the camera may be blocked in a variety of different ways.

Additionally, unscrupulous officers may intentionally interfere with the recording in a variety of different ways. When any of this happens during an incident of interest to the public, a cloud of suspicion may appear over both the officers involved and the agency. The Department of Justice and the Office of Community Oriented Policing Services sponsored a study (2012-CK-WX-K028) that recommends that agencies educate their community and courts on the limitations and operational challenges associated with body-worn cameras. It is reasonable to think that in some cases it will simply be assumed that the officer intentionally did something to prevent the recording for nefarious reasons, regardless of what actually caused it to fail. Take the example from August of 2015 where an Officer in Tuscaloosa, Alabama, shot and killed a man after a struggle. In this case, the officer failed to activate his body camera. On August 25th, 5 days after the shooting and with no information as to why the camera was not activated, activist and blogger Shaun King wrote on the popular American political blog Daily Kos, "This is a highly disturbing fact and calls into question every choice the officer made that day" (King 2015: para 4). In the eyes of some, the officer has already been found guilty of excessive force simply because footage of the shooting did not exist. This circumstance can be more damaging to an agency's credibility than if an agency did not have the camera at all.

Implementation of clear and thorough policies can go a long way to address these issues. Popular or not these policy mandates can include officers notifying citizens when they are being recorded and editing requirements for when agencies publically release a recording that contains explicit or inappropriate images. In much the same way as policy requires use, policies can also mandate simple documentation procedures for when cameras fail to ensure that an agency can illustrate to the public and to the courts that these devices sometimes fail through no fault of the officer. This will help establish that it wasn't just "this time" that the technology failed. As noted by Bain in Chapter 4, and as Laine (2009) has stated elsewhere, open and candid communication with the public is an imperative. The same can be said about the use of technology, its capabilities and limitations, which can also serve to address these types of issues. Where trials with body-worn cameras have been ongoing, both in the United States and in the United Kingdom, findings are still rather limited. However, a study by Ariel, Farrar and Sutherland (2014), has found that where the born-worn cameras are in use it is providing for substantial reductions in both use of force incidents and citizen complaints, which is of great importance as we move forward, and plan for their implementation. The findings were reported in the November, 2014 *Journal of Quantitative Criminology* and were the first of its type in the United States.

One final consideration related to body-worn cameras is likely to be what a budget minded person may see as a duplication of service. More bluntly, why pay for the more expensive in-car camera systems if we can rely on the less expensive body-worn cameras? It will be incumbent upon the agency administrator to inform those making the funding decisions about a few basic differences between the two recording systems. First, is the issue of triggers. In-car camera systems can be set to automatically activate based on a number of variables such as speed, emergency equipment use, and impact or force. In many cases, this guarantees activation of the system at a time when it should be activated. At this time, body-worn cameras have to be manually activated by the officer. Second, many in-car camera recording systems have the option of rear seat recording, or the ability to record the prisoner in the car at the same time the forward facing camera is recording. This is not a capability of body-worn cameras, but it is an important consideration in terms of prisoner transportation liability. A body-worn camera simply sees what the officer sees, nothing more. Finally, there are options for data to appear on the recording of the incident. This valuable data, such as time and date, method of activation, speed of the vehicle and GPS location can automatically be contained in the video and it is not subject to the relatively short battery life of a body-worn camera, which at times may fail, and at no fault of the officer.

In-car camera recording systems have been part of the law enforcement landscape much longer than body-worn cameras, making their use much more common. Some of the same concerns that exist with body-worn cameras exist with these systems, but their capability and limitations are much more familiar to the general public simply because of their longer history of use. Over time and with the education of the general public, agencies may enjoy the same public familiarity with body-worn cameras.

The Power to Subdue

The nature of law enforcement is such that sometimes it is necessary to physically engage someone for the purpose of gaining compliance, taking someone into custody, or even keeping that person safe from themselves. Over the years a variety of tools have been used to assist in this aspect of the job ranging from night sticks and pepper spray, to collapsible batons and weapons of opportunity found at hand. As with most technology advancements, improvements continued to be made. Today, officers make use of some of the best technology available for this purpose, electronic control devices (ECD).

Electronic control devices are a technology that came to law enforcement in the early 1990's and their use is now widespread. As with body-worn cameras, they provide considerable benefit to law enforcement, but in much the same way, their implementation and use should be carefully considered by law enforcement agencies. Although their use has been widely reported to reduce an agency's cost by virtue of fewer officer and suspect injuries, cost associated with purchase, replacement, and training have to be assured for the long term. Electronic control devices are not inexpensive, nor is it inexpensive to maintain department wide certification. Paying for the officer's time, the trainer's time, the training equipment, it all adds up very quickly.

Electronic control devices can generally be used in two fashions. One involves pain compliance, and one involves neuromuscular incapacitation. Both are generally effective. One of the concerns, however, with many law enforcement administrators is the over reliance of the ECD by officers, and they, as with any technology, sometimes fail. One illustration is provided by the April 4th, 2013 edition of policemag.com where police in Marysville, Washington, deployed an electronic control device on a suspect who was freely running about Interstate 5. They deployed the ECD four times with seemingly no affect. It wasn't until a fourth officer arrived that police were able to subdue the suspect. Were the officers too reliant on the ECD? Should officers have moved to other intermediate options such as a baton, or chemical spray after the initial failures? What if the encounter took place with an agency who didn't have four officers to respond to a call of this nature? Does the agency provide the officer with enough tools and training to do without the ECD if those circumstances present? If so, can the same be said of all officers?

There is also the concern that officers may over utilize ECDs as an effective and expeditious tool for dealing with an uncooperative suspect. In an article by Dr. Ron Martinelli, an expert in police practice with Martinelli and Associates, he refers to this overreliance on electronic control devices as "Taser Mentality." He defines this as

...a conscious or unconscious over-reliance on the Taser to defend, control or generate compliance of an encountered subject absent those factors or circumstances that would lead a "reasonable officer" to believe that the subject posed a threat by active resistance or violent behavior

Martinelli 2009: 1–2

He cautions police administrators on implementing policies that address this issue and ensure that other skills, such as physical capability and the ability to effectively communicate do not go by the wayside. These types of issues, however, can be addressed through a well-developed training program, training above and beyond the basic certification. Currently, after initial certification, annual training requirements are very limited and are largely satisfied by deploying two cartridges into a stationary target. To realize the full benefit of ECDs, it's not good enough to certify an officer on the use of an ECD and simply conduct the annual recertification. To be effective tools, ECDs should be included in scenario based training and scenarios should reflect the reality that they will sometimes fail and an officer should quickly turn to another weapon choice or tactic. Had this been the case in the example from Marysville (WA) described earlier, the outcome may have been somewhat different.

An agency administrator will also have to determine if the agency can afford to issue an ECD to each officer, or will they be supplied to each officer at the start of their shift. If each officer is issued one, are they permitted to be carried off-duty? Will they be permitted to use them when they provide police services off-duty, such as non-department paid security details? Will all of the same protections be in place or required for officers using them off-duty, such as body-worn cameras? As you can see, it is not as simple as purchasing the product and handing them out to officers. All of these issues should be considered and addressed prior to the implementation of an ECD program.

CAMERA PHONES AND SOCIAL MEDIA

The video that illustrates the failure of the ECD on Highway 5 in Marysville, Washington, that was previously mentioned in this chapter also illustrates another technological issue that law enforcement deals with on a regular basis; camera phones and social media.

The advent of social media has been a blessing and a curse to many law enforcement administrators. Many agencies have successfully used various social media both to assist in criminal investigations and to further public relation efforts. Thus, by utilizing the services in the way described by Robinson (see Chapter 5), police agencies have the opportunity to gather important knowledge from the local community, and appropriately frame information, instantly providing it for the public. Whether it's information about a traffic concern, a crime or community event, as Robinson has noted (see Chapter 5), social media serves to enhance the ability of law enforcement to communicate directly with the public. However, effective use of department social media is not as easy as it may sound.

Long before a department engages social media, serious consideration needs to be given to a number of concerns. Would any agency administrator allow just any employee to talk to the media about a department issue? When designating who in the agency has access to department social media and what they are permitted to post, an agency administrator has to accept that whatever is posted becomes the department's position (on the issue) and is no different from communicating that information to the news media. Careful consideration has to be given to the development of policy that surrounds the use of department social media by individuals authorized to use it. Some of those considerations should include compliance with public record law restrictions and exceptions, how to address issues that are political in nature, and the nature and amount of information that will be posted to social media. Any advice provided on social media should be well vetted and consistent with best practices. What gets posted to social media should be treated no differently than a press release, because ultimately, the end result is the same, minus the middle man. Agencies need to decide if and how they will allow the public to comment or post to their social media. If commenting is permitted, decisions regarding what is appropriate and what is not appropriate have to be made in advance to allow for consistent and routine application of those rules.

Finally, if the public is going to be permitted to post to the departments social media, will the media be monitored on a 24-hour a day, 7-day a week basis to avoid inappropriate or embarrassing posts? It should be remembered that the public can also frame information and get it instantly to the masses. These are all concerns and issues that an administrator needs to be aware of prior to making the decision to make use of social media in the name of the department or agency. Social media can certainly benefit the communication efforts of a police department, but it is also easy to see the many negative implications if not carefully managed. Thus, where Robinson talks of 5-star rating systems, it is easy to see how this may be corrupted by thoughtless or poor use of such a service.

Another concern separate from department social media is personal social media accounts used by officers who have access to department information. Do you allow officers to post pictures that they took while on duty, seemingly innocuous crime scene photos, or traffic accidents? Do you allow them to comment on department operations or to be publicly critical of the administration? These are all questions that require careful consideration, both legal and otherwise, before the development of policy that allows an administration to control this type of information. Failure to address these issues could result in something similar to the controversy that took place in Indiana in 2009 when an Indiana State Trooper posted pictures of himself with an Indianapolis police officer pointing a gun at his head while at a party. The same trooper also referred to himself as a garbage man, because, he says, "I pick up garbage for a living" (Segall 2009). Neither of these incidents are likely to gain the favor of the community these officers serve and likely had a negative impact on the public view of each department. While there is some guidance relative to case law and existing public record laws, what gets posted to social media by employees is largely up to the individual agency to decide and monitor.

While having accurate and timely information can generally be considered a good thing, the question also arises whether there can be too much information made available, too quickly. The answer, of course, is yes. It will be up to the agency administrator to address the concerns in the way that is best for the individual community.

BATTLEFIELD TECHNOLOGY

Related to having too much information, or at least more information than we ever had before, is the use and data collection capabilities of unmanned aerial vehicles, or drones. The recent wars in the Middle East have revealed this new and impressive technology to the general public. Drones are common place in many military operations and have proven to be an effective technology on the battlefield. Can they also be an effective technology for law enforcement?

Until recently, only large agencies with substantial resources could have aviation assets at their disposal. Helicopter or fixed wing aircraft for surveillance or enforcement purposes was an expensive proposition. The advent of drones, however, have put this technology, on a smaller scale, in the hands of everyday citizens. To be clear, we are not talking about weaponized unmanned aircraft that fly over 100 miles an hour at 25,000 feet. We are however, talking about a technology that can give the user an unprecedented eye in the sky, for good and bad.

Can aerial capabilities be an asset to law enforcement? Of course they can. Should a law enforcement agency carefully consider the implications prior to administering such a program? Absolutely they should. As discussed previously, privacy issues are the number one concern when it comes to this and any technology. Generally, the Supreme Court has held that you do not have an expectation of privacy in a public place, but what about in your own backyard? Are you shielded from law enforcement's eye in the sky when it is not over or on your property? We know that the Supreme Court extends the most Fourth Amendment protection to the home. Does anyone want the government, law enforcement or not, viewing activities just outside our homes? Should an agency be concerned with the public perception implication from drone use? This will be different from community to community and is something that should be carefully deliberated.

Under what circumstances would an agency permit drone use? Missing persons? High crime areas or drug activity surveillance? Rush hour traffic monitoring? Any time an operator feels it appropriate to fly it? Policies and procedures that are consistent with current law and balance the individual's privacy rights would be necessary. After the events of Ferguson (MO), and Baltimore (MD), and the belief that local police have become too militarized, the benefits of this type of technology should be heavily weighed against the potentially negative perception by the public and the potential loss of public support.

Another issue that is important to consider when discussing the use of drones by law enforcement is safety. In most cases, law enforcement's use of drones is going to involve flying over people and occupied structures. As with any aerial vehicle, crashes will occur. Despite the best safety efforts, there will still be accidents, either resulting from equipment malfunction or pilot error. When this happens, there could be costly loss of equipment, property damage, and, most concerning, injury to people. A recent example of such an incident was in 2014 when the Montgomery County Sheriff's Office in Texas lost a $250,000 drone to Lake Conroe after an apparent malfunction during a training exercise (Alexander 2014). Nearly 2 years prior to that, the same agency suffered a similar incident when a prototype drone crashed into a police tactical vehicle during a photo opportunity (Hill 2012). And, although not an example from a law enforcement drone, drones do hurt people on the ground. In September 2015, debris from a drone that had fallen to the ground caused injury to the head of an 11-month-old child who was in a stroller near Pasadena City Hall. It is believed that the signal from the controller to the drone was lost causing the drone to crash (Henry 2015). Because accidents will most certainly happen, decision makers must weigh the risk of agency drone use against the benefits provided by the use of the drone. These decisions will either have to be spelled out in operational policy or made on a case by case basis.

What must also be considered in this type of technology is the obvious use by those that perpetrate crime in the first place. This has been seen most recently in the state of Ohio, where it was reported in the Columbus Dispatch on August 15th, 2015, that a Mansfield, Ohio, prison yard drone drop of illegal drugs was the not first time the Ohio prison system experienced such an incident (Ludlow 2015).

Drones can provide enormous information gathering benefit and provide capabilities that we once could only have imagined. But, as our Founding Fathers made explicit in the Fourth Amendment, and as illustrated by many Supreme Court decisions, a high value is placed on individual privacy rights. This is a concept that must be respected by law enforcement if we are ultimately to be successful in defending the Constitution, as we are sworn to do.

(Digital) Records Management Systems

From the oldest veteran to the youngest officer and everyone in between, it is widely accepted that if it isn't documented, it didn't happen. The importance of documentation is an undeniable fact of law enforcement. Daily logs, e-mails, and incident reports are just a few examples of some ways that we document information and activity. Even in circumstances where paperwork is actually still paper, some agencies digitize those documents and store them on a server or in the cloud. In-car camera footage, body camera footage, crime scene photographs, recordings from interviews, interrogations and a variety of other proceedings are also records that need to be stored. Digital records are more common today than ever before. Their use saves space, virtually guarantees storage if properly done and makes retrieval a simple process. But, digital records management systems are some of the most complicated technologies that any administrator will have to consider.

It is never as simple as just purchasing the software and moving forward digitally. In a perfect world, all of your digital data platforms within your agency will be linked and able to communicate with each other. In an even more perfect world, those same systems would be able to communicate with other agencies and organizations which you routinely share information. In this digital age, ideally, everything is able to communicate with everything else. Will your records management system (RMS) communicate with your computer aided dispatch system? Is the RMS system able to be connected to an e-ticketing solution? Is your in-car camera and body-worn camera video able to be uploaded into your RMS? Are there proprietary issues? Is your RMS hosted on your own server, or is it hosted in the cloud? If it is in the cloud, do you own the data? If it only exists on a server, do you have sufficient backups in place in the event of a disaster or even a simple systems crash? Do you have sufficient storage?

This is not intended to be a barrage of questions to shy someone away from the use of these technologies, but it is intended to be an illustration of mistakes that have been made over the years by many law enforcement agencies. This is unfortunately an unforgiving arena where it is critically important to have the technological foresight to ask the right questions during the planning and selection phase. If you do not have the foresight within your agency, it is something that should be sought from outside the agency. The consequence for not doing so could mean that an agency incurs the full cost of implementing this technology, but doesn't realize nearly its full potential.

Issues in Data Protection

While there are many issues to consider related to records management and digital storage, the most important issue may very well be data protection. Law enforcement agencies collect and maintain large amounts of information, and sometimes that information can be derogatory, compromising, or outright embarrassing for an individual or even an organization. With pending investigations, unauthorized release of information can compromise the investigation or even create a risk of safety to officers and persons involved. While some information will become public record at some point, often times at the adjudication of a criminal case, some records will never reach that status. Each law enforcement agency has an obligation to responsibly manage that information and prevent it from public release. To be clear, we are not talking about a "King George" approach to the people's records, we are talking about information that should be protected. For example, consider someone who is alleged to have committed a child sex crime, a very serious and disturbing allegation. The allegation is investigated and ultimately there is not enough probable cause to warrant a criminal charge. As a matter of fact, it's unclear if the suspect even committed the act that they were alleged to have committed, or if it was a personal vendetta being settled with a false allegation. In most cases, with a private citizen, a law enforcement agency would not identify that person as the suspect in a crime if they did not have the probable cause to charge them. Irreparable damage could be caused to the person's reputation and the person's family, when the allegation may not even be in fact true. Under Ohio public records law, Ohio Revised Code section 149.3(A)(1)(h), those records, or any records tending to reveal the identity of an uncharged suspect, are exempt from public release for that reason. While this is an extreme example, it is one illustration of the need to protect data that is collected by the police. Anyone with a computer knows of the need to protect themselves from hackers and those who would attempt to steal their personal information. Police departments must address this with capable information technology providers. But, what happens when the intrusion comes from within? Unfortunately, this is not an unwarranted concern and there are plenty of examples of it happening. Two law suits have been filed against the Las Vegas Police Department for information that officers provided to a private investigator that they were not authorized to release. Court papers allege that officers "continuously and systematically gave him access to confidential and proprietary information of citizens of the state of Nevada without their knowledge or consent" (Green 2009: para 6). Another example comes from Franklin, Tennessee where in 2014 a deputy chief was suspended and demoted for releasing information from a pending investigation which was not authorized to be released and jeopardized the investigation (Horne 2014).

There is also the issue of lost or destroyed data, data that is likely to be evidence. CNBC reported that Eastern European hackers have hit police departments nationwide with "ransomware" demanding ransoms in lieu of destroying files after an encryption prevents police access. Departments in seven states since 2013 have suffered these attacks (Francescani 2016).

There are many examples of data breaches that have occurred with people's personal data and law enforcement data. Sometimes those breaches take place internally through unauthorized access by employees who may release it or use it for personal gain, and sometimes it comes externally by way of criminal hacking as we have seen in many cases. From an internal standpoint, policies and procedures and accountability measures are necessary to protect that information. In addition to having policies and procedures that identify who can release information and under what circumstances, an agency needs the ability to audit digital records and activity and know who accesses information. When information is compromised, can the agency administrator point to the rule that was violated and can they identify, through digital audit, who violated it? If not, data is at risk. From an external standpoint, whether you store in the cloud or on a local server, is that data protected from the outside? Do you have security measures in place to prevent a hacker from accessing that information? Obviously these technical issues are going to be the responsibility of the agency's information technology providers, but it's the responsibility of the police chief or administrator to ensure that it happens. Without accountability in this regard, it would be difficult to ensure data protection or address it when it happens.

SUMMARY

For an officer like the one mentioned at the beginning of this chapter, it would not be difficult to understand his lack of interest in technology advances. What we are doing today in law enforcement is starkly different than what was done just 25 years ago and certainly more so than 50 years ago. Technology has undoubtedly benefited this profession in very substantial and meaningful ways, as Bain, Mackey and Courtney, Conser and Carsone, and Robinson, have all noted at varying stages in the text. However, it has also been expensive, complicated, time consuming, frustrating and sometimes not at all what we expected it to be. For an agency to benefit the most from any of the technology advances available to law enforcement they must become intimately familiar with both the good and the bad and ensure that both are taken into consideration when decisions are made, and when planning and implementation are undertaken.

REFERENCES

Alexander, H. (2014, April 30). $250 police drone crashes into Lake Conroe. *The Houston Chronical.* Available at: http://www.chron.com/neighborhood/wood lands/article/250K-police-drone-crashes-into-Lake-Conroe-5435343.php.

Ariel, B., Farrar, W. A., & Sutherland, A. (2014). The effect of police body-worn cameras on use of force and citizens' complaints against the police: A randomized controlled trial. *Journal of Quantitative Criminology, 31*(3), 509–535.

Berman, M., & Horwitz, S. (2015, May 1). Justice Dept. will spend $20 million on police body cameras nationwide. *Washington Post*. Available at: https://www.washingtonpost.com/news/post-nation/wp/2015/05/01/justice-dept-to-help-police-agencies-across-the-country-get-body-cameras/.

Department of Justice. (2012). Implementing a body worn camera program. Recommendations and lessons learned. 2012-CK-WX-K028. Available at: www.justice.gov/iso/opa/resources/472014912134715246869.pdf.

Francescani, C. (2016, April 26). Ransomware hackers blackmail U.S. police departments. CNBC. Available at: http://www.cnbc.com/2016/04/26/ransomware-hackers-blackmail-us-police-departments.html.

Green, S. (2009, November 17). Suit filed over officer's release of unauthorized information. *The Las Vegas Sun*. Available at: http://www.lasvegassun.com/news/2009/nov/17/suit-filed-over-officers-release-unauthorized-info/.

Griffith, D (2015, May 24). Kings of the Road. *Police Technology*. Available at: http://www.policemag.com/channel/technology/articles/2015/05/kings-of-the-road.aspx.

Henry, J. (2015, September 15). Fallen drone injures 11-month old near Pasadena City Hall. *The Pasadena Star-News*. Available at: http://www.pasadenastarnews.com/general-news/20150915/falling-drone-injures-11-month-old-near-pasadena-city-hall.

Hill, K. (2012, March 1). The drone that crashed into a S.W.A.T. teams tank. *Forbes*. Available at http://www.forbes.com/sites/kashmirhill/2012/03/05/the-drone-that-crashed-into-a-s-w-a-t-teams-tank/#24fda23d5e19.

Horne, P. (2014, January 25). FPD veteran employee demoted from deputy chief to lieutenant: Rahinsky. *The Herald*. Available at: http://www.williamsonherald.com/sports/article_0931afdc-e37d-5b18-8f8c-35dd24ece45b.html.

King, S. (2015, August 25). Alabama police admit officer's body camera was turned off before shooting man holding spoon. Available at: http://www.dailykos.com/story/2015/8/25/1415297/-Alabama-police-admit-officer-turned-off-body-camera-before-shooting-man-holding-spoon.

Laine, R. (2009). Law enforcement and public perception: Race, ethnicity, and community policing. *The Police Chief, 76*(9). [electronic] Available at: http://www.policechiefmagazine.org/magazine/index.cfm?fuseaction=display&article_id=1883&issue_id=92009.

Ludlow, R. (2015, August 15). Mansfield prison drone drug drop not the first in Ohio this year, Columbus dispatch. Available at: http://www.dispatch.com/content/stories/local/2015/08/14/drone-drug-drop-ohio-prison.html.

Martinelli, R. (2009). Taser ® ECD mentality. Available at: http://www.martinelliandassoc.com/pdf/Taser_Mentality-final.pdf.

NIJ. (2014, March 18). Perceptions of treatment by Police. *Race, Trust and Police Legitimacy.* Available at: http://nij.gov/topics/law-enforcement/legitimacy/Pages/perceptions.aspx.

Segall, B. (2009, March 25). Trooper in trouble over Facebook photos. Available at: http://www.wthr.com/story/10066071/trooper-in-trouble-over-facebook-photos.

Weitzer, R., & Tuch, S. A. (2005). Determinants of public satisfaction with the police. *Police Quarterly, 8*(3), 279–297.

Andrew Turowski is the Chief of Police for the City of Louisville (Ohio). He has 24 years of police experience with assignments to patrol, investigations, the Stark County Metropolitan narcotics unit, a FBI Violent Crimes Fugitive Task Force, and a FBI Joint Terrorism Task Force. He also served in the U.S. Army Military Police Corps. He is a member of the Ohio Association of Chiefs of Police where he is a Certified Law Enforcement Executive (CLEE). He has a Master's Degree in Public Administration and serves as an adjunct professor at Kent State University and the University of Mount Union.

CHAPTER 8

Technology and the Future of Policing

*Andy Bain, Louis P. Carsone, James A. Conser,
Brandon J. Courtney, William J. Mackey, Bryan K. Robinson
and Andrew Turowski*

(All authors had equal participation in the writing of this chapter and names appear in alphabetical order)

A. Bain (✉) · B.K. Robinson
Department of Sociology and Criminal Justice, University of Mount Union, Alliance, OH, USA
e-mail: bainaj@mountunion.edu; robinsbk@mountunion.edu

L.P. Carsone
Department of Public Safety, Hubbard, OH, USA
e-mail: bluejet514@neo.rr.com

J.A. Conser
Department of Sociology and Criminal Justice, University of Mount Union, Alliance, OH, USA
Department of Criminal Justice and Forensic Science, Youngstown State University, Youngstown, OH, USA
e-mail: theconsers@frontier.com or jaconser@ysu.edu

B.J. Courtney
Department of English, Passaic County Community College, Paterson, NJ, USA
e-mail: brandon.james.courtney@gmail.com

W.J. Mackey
Department of Criminology, Indiana State University, Terre Haute, IN, USA
e-mail: william.mackey@indstate.edu

A. Turowski
Chief of Police, Louisville Police Department, Louisville, Ohio, USA
e-mail: turowsan@mountunion.edu or aturowsk@kent.edu

© The Author(s) 2016   115
A. Bain (ed.), *Law Enforcement and Technology*,
DOI 10.1057/978-1-137-57915-7_8

Abstract In this final chapter the authors have come together to present a brief discussion of the future of technology, its use by law enforcement officers/officials, and its potential concern. The technology under development today will soon reach the "street" tomorrow and the timeframe from development to common usage is becoming shorter in this digital age. This final chapter is, without doubt, an extremely important discussion to have. As the introduction to this text stated, the pace of change that takes place in technology today has never been seen before, and to maintain our knowledge and understanding, we need to be forward thinking and innovative in our own use of technology.

Keywords Future challenges · Possible future scenarios · Technology advances

The Future

The future of policing has been the focus of many articles and studies in recent years (e.g., Conser and Frissora 2007; Schafer 2007; Scherer and Jarvis 2011; Treverton et al. 2011; McCullough and Spence 2012; Wakefield 2013; Accenture 2013; Police Executive Research Forum 2014; Newcombe 2014; Silberglitt et al. 2015). Most textbooks on policing and/or law enforcement also contain at least one chapter on the future of the field.

As we see it, the future of police technology is twofold: on the one hand, technology offers myriad possibilities for apprehension, investigation, surveillance, and less-than-lethal force, all of which offer more exactitude and precision. On the other, it can result in many more questions than we presently have answers to. These questions may include constitutional issues, notwithstanding privacy and data ownership agreements and arguments, but they may also include issues concerning individual rights and responsibilities.

What comes to mind when a person is asked to think of the future? Do they contemplate what the future holds for them as an individual (i.e., a job/career, salary/wealth, family, retirement) or what the future holds for society (i.e., crime, overall economy, war/conflict, prosperity, and globalization)? In addressing the first of these two points – that of the future – we must start with the latter.

The focus of this text is technology, but that is only one driver of potential change in the future – there are many other influential factors that shape our futures (plural, because there are many possible futures). These other social factors/drivers may include demographics, economic, ecological, political, legal, and cultural. The following table illustrates some of the trends and issues within each of these drivers. The items listed under each driver are not exhaustive, they are examples; and one should view Table 8.1 as dynamic, more as a Rubik's Cube, and not linear as you could expect of a chain of events one preceding the next.

For example, one can ask questions about any jurisdiction in the United States or any other country regarding these environmental drivers: How prepared are the police for a natural disaster? Racial unrest? Cyber-attack? Terrorist attack? Prison escape? Resettlement of thousands of refugees? Economic collapse – runs on banks? The scenarios and the predictions are somewhat limitless, but still bear some discussion.

In 1984, authors Carsone and Conser published an article on the day in the life of patrol officers (Field Agents) and supervisors in the future. Their scenario included the vision of:

- Voice recognition computers
- Talking computers
- Robotic jailors
- Real-time Field Agent status screens
- Solar-powered Emergency Transport Vehicles with voice command and self-driving features
- Accident Avoidance vehicles
- Automatic dispatching of required appearance calls
- Background analysis of all contacts and dispatched calls
- Personal protection field sensors with real-time monitoring of heartbeat and respiration
- Automated backup based on field sensors
- Automatic submission of all reports
- Need for management foresight

Although the technology exists for all of their vision, the Carsone/Conser scenario has not yet totally come to fruition in the 30 (plus) years since writing, but we are confident it won't take too many more years to accomplish the remainder. The Motorola Company has envisioned "smartbelts" and "smartglasses" as tools for officers, but which could

Table 8.1 Environmental drivers that affect the future

Demographics	Economics	Ecological	Political	Technological	Legal	Cultural
Immigration	Poverty	Climate shifts	Political unrest	Body-cameras	Privacy issues	Diversity/Multiculturalism
Migration trends	Unemployment	Pollution	Civil disobedience	Drones/UAS	Supreme Court rulings	Multi-Language society
Aging population	Minimum wage	Natural disasters	Distrust of government	Surveillance technology	Federal laws & regulation	Assimilation
Ethnicity	Underemployment	Food production	Terror attack	Crime analysis	State laws	Changing values
Multiple jurisdictions	Agency resources	Water resources	Liberal policies	Agency resources	Drug decriminalization	Crime rates
Educational levels	Federal grants	Seasonal changes	Conservative policies	Cyber crime	Liability	Stigma of offenders
Class structure and conflict	Fiscal policy	Diseases	Libertarian policies	Forensic science advances	"Law lag"	Religion

also be used to send an instant message to dispatch regarding an officers location – with GPS coordinates. In addition, the smartbelt could be fitted with technology that senses when the officer retrieves a piece of critical equipment (handcuffs, taser, gun, etc.), and then have the "smartglasses" take photographs through an automated system, and which is then able to send directly to police headquarters in real time. Dispatchers can also send the officer text messages that would display on the lenses of the glasses, so that the officer can receive the information without looking away from the scene (Madhani 2015).

It is envisioned that with the high-profile shootings of law enforcement officers in 2015 and again in 2016, that officer safety is going to be built-in to much of the personal technology for officers. Sensors to detect nearby persons (movement and weapons detection), panoramic surveillance on headgear or glasses, and real-time data transmission to communication centers are believed to be future priorities. When the above is coupled with 360-degree vehicle cameras, GPS locator systems, and unmanned aircraft systems, we can envision quicker response to officer-involved situations. Advances in less-than-lethal technology will continue, however, if per-fected, there is no guarantee that this will reduce deadly attacks against officers. It may actually increase the attacks as an unintended consequence since the offender knows they will not be seriously injured; and if they succeed in their attack, they will have access to the officer's latest technology.

Taking a look at additional technologies that are in use today, viewing those technologies as building blocks, and mentally "building" new solu-tions from the blocks, might give an even clearer glimpse of some of the possible futures for law enforcement. Consider the following technology items that either exist today or are in development.

Other Technologies Include:

- Google has recently released an app that allows users to upload photos to its cloud and search them for the presence of objects or particular faces, among other things (Hernandez 2015).
- PlateSmart is advertising a software-only system that, working with an existing computer and in-car camera systems, provides a License Plate Recognition System (PlateSmart n.d.).
- Predictive Policing Software can aid small police departments as well as large ones. Most police departments use some form of a

computerized records management system. Capturing detailed data and having the appropriate software, the data can be analyzed and the analysis used to predict when and where particular types of incidents can be expected to occur. Some software can generate maps displaying various data (Galvin 2015).

You may recall from previous chapters that today we not only discuss the possibilities of body-worn cameras, but have begun to accept them as a reality in today's policing methods. However, systems already exist which allow for a live, encrypted, video feed to be transmitted to a command center. Additionally, it is also possible to transmit GPS information. This provides the command center personnel the ability to see and hear what is transpiring. The GPS data can be displayed "onto a dynamic map creating an unprecedented situation overview for the team leaders" (A watching brief with body-worn devices 2007: 7). This is not so much about the future, but what can be done right now, and as you may have picked up upon, it is an article from 2007, making it almost a decade old. The article closes with the words; "The possibilities are endless . . . " (ibid.), and they are.

But, before looking at those endless possibilities, a few more *building block* realities can be considered. For example, an advertisement about the 2016 Ford Police Interceptor Utility vehicle describes a system whereby surveillance technology can detect someone approaching from the rear of the vehicle, and then raise the driver's window and lock all doors (Advertisement 2015: 4).

A report submitted to the Department of Justice described research on an intelligent video system with the purpose of detecting and preventing both criminal and disorderly activities (Krahnstoever 2011). The intent of the research was the development of a system that could analyze social interaction among groups and detect the onset of potentially dangerous activities, such as assault. This was accomplished through the use of a network of automatically controlled cameras, facial recognition technology, and a system for analyzing group structures. The development of such technology, says Krahnstoever (2011: 1), "can help law enforcement detect many different types of activities and alert operators in many cases about the onset of an event – enabling early detection and possibly prevention of critical events."

Pursuant to recommendations of the 9/11 Commission, Congress created FirstNet, which is the First Responder Network Authority. One goal of FirstNet is to allow first responders "to take advantage of evolving, Internet-based mobile communications technology through intelligent devices like smartphones and tablets, as well as wearable technology" (Kennedy 2015: 24). FirstNet, says Kennedy (2015), would provide a public safety network that, in an emergency, would not be overloaded as a commercial network may be.

Additional services we could see include the development of in wind-shield displays, referred to as HuDs (Heads-up Displays) in order to provide the officer with all of the information they need in order to aid the travel to the scene, but also to alert them to any possible dangers. However, as with all things, there is some research which suggests that HuDs can act as an additional driver distraction, and requires much more sensory energy from the driver of the vehicle than a vehicle with no such technology (Gitlin 2015).

A non-technical technique that is taught to some police officers involves the development of a good intuition about people and situations based upon their actions, individually or collectively, their body language, and their speech patterns. Non-verbal indicators may warn an officer that an attack, or other dangerous action by a subject, is imminent (Glennon 2008; Sancier 2012). Perhaps a police body-worn camera could be "taught" to look for such indicators.

CONCERNS

Just with all the good to come, there are a myriad of concerns, questions, and issues by this type of technology-related speculation. Among those is officer appearance. As more technology becomes available in body-worn format, what will the police officer of the near future look like? Will the technology lead to the police looking like a Robo-Cop with helmet, heads-up display visor, exterior body armor, and flashing sensors (as depicted in Paul Verhoeven's 1987 movie of the same name)? A further concern is whether or not the police will come to look like an occupying, futuristic army in a hostile land, as has previously been discussed by Kraska and Kappeler (1997), and Kraska (2007)? Or, will the technology be "built into" a softer presentation uniform?

Another concern is the amount of data that can be generated and thrown at an officer. Even with some type of a heads-up display and audio sent to an ear-bud, how much data can an officer be expected to process? One possible solution would be to use technology to monitor the data generated by the technology. However, this seems a little like overkill, having technologies designed specifically to monitor other technologies.

Perhaps an on-board (body-worn) computer could be programmed with a police department's policy, data on body language and facial expressions, voice inflections, and images of weapons. Then, as the various technological items (body-cameras, body microphones, forward looking infrared, and precision metal detectors, for example) scan the environment, a computer could make the decisions on warning a subject to back away, stop, or take his/her hands out of pockets. If the subject refused to listen, and other parameters were met, perhaps we could allow the computer to deploy a less-lethal weapon such as an electro-stun device or pepper spray. The computer could then assemble all of the data leading up to the decision, and prepare the report. Perhaps the police officer will simply become a tool of the computer. In other words, will we rule the technology, or will we allow the technology to rule us?

On the other hand, heavy reliance on police technology carries with it a number of problematic questions. First, who owns the countless amounts of data and processed information? We cannot dismiss the possibility that companies may try to lay claim to data collected through their devices. This has been an ongoing problem with cellular companies and carriers, cable and internet providers, television manufacturers, and a league of other technological industries (Pepitone 2013; Krebs 2015). Added to this is the complicating fact that there are certain guarantees of (individual) privacy as set down in the U.S. Constitution (4th Amendment), providing for protection from unreasonable searches and seizures, whilst at the same time providing for a reasonable expectation of privacy (Farb 2002); and the *Privacy Act (1974)*, which "…seeks to regulate personal data processing… It regulates the collection, use, and disclosure of all types of personal information, by all types of federal agencies, including law enforcement agencies" (Bignami 2015: 5). Equally problematic would be a catastrophic data breach. We are all too familiar with the vulnerability of data, especially concerning malicious actors who seek to use our personal information and data to their benefit (Sen and Borle 2015). Advanced security, then, becomes a requirement: we need to be more sophisticated and reliable than our current safeguards would seem to allow for.

Equally important is the reliance on the accuracy of the network of technological devices used by the police in the field. Our society relies heavily on the integration of technologies, or "The Internet of Things" (for a full discussion of this concept see: Hollywood et al. 2015), a general term recently coined for creating a complex network of "smart" or connected items; furthermore, we expect these technologies to perform at an increasingly decisive and unequivocal level. But what happens when, as is often the case, these technologies fail or perform to a less than precise level? Such failures can occur with measurably limited likelihood for a single piece of technology, but when creating a network of multiple items – each giving and relaying information to the others – it can exponentially increase the potential for failure. In our daily lives, a random failure of one of our connected items can be, at worst, frustrating. The same failure could prove catastrophic, however, in the field.

THE POSITIVE SENSE OF TECHNOLOGY

While disaster scenarios are easy to imagine, it is imperative to also examine the tangential positives of these technologies. For instance, the recent accusations of officers being more likely to use force against minority suspects would be greatly reduced, if not eliminated through the use of multiple video feeds. Second, the seemingly constant need for greater numbers of officers on the street would be considerably eased, as each officer (fully equipped with up-to-date technology) could do the work of multiple, unequipped units. Perhaps most useful, however, would be a kind of uniformity of behavior for both police and the citizens with whom they interact. Currently, each citizen and each officer carry their own ideas of acceptable, harmful, or threatening behaviors. For one officer, they may interpret an inebriated man's angry rants as harmless and a symptom of simple drunkenness. Another officer, however, may interpret the same individual as a threat, and act with force. By having a programmed response to specific behaviors and actions, both police and citizens could have, at the very least, a more solid foundation for the potential repercussions of their actions.

The rise of social media presents both new challenges and new solutions for the future of policing. As recent research suggests public opinions of law enforcement may play a significant role in perceptions of public safety and overall fear of crime (see Bain et al. 2014). Consequently, if tools like Twitter are effectively harnessed by the law enforcement community they can help alleviate social tensions between the police and citizens as well as address public concerns of safety (Lytle and Randa 2015). Social media tools provide one possible solution for improving agency relationships with the local community. However, if social media tools are ignored by the law enforcement community at best they will have missed an opportunity to improve public relations and at worst they may find more and more disenfranchised groups using social media to organize against and even disrupt law enforcement activities – as was seen to take place in London during the 2011 riots, and again in Baltimore in the summer of 2015. However, this latter event saw a much more coordinated attempt by law enforcement officials to try to use social media to help alleviate public concerns and criticism. Indeed, the report Social Media and Tactical Considerations for Law Enforcement, by the office for Community Orientated Policing Services (Melekain and Wexler 2013: iii) has noted that " ... police departments are developing many new technologies that have the potential to make policing more efficient and effective" and continue, stating that "Social media can be counted as one of these important new technologies."

As the demand for oversight and accountability increases in a post-Ferguson era social media provides an outlet through which both law enforcement agencies and everyday citizens can instantaneously disseminate information to the masses. Many researchers have lauded the positive outcomes of community policing practices and as our society becomes more entrenched in the digital world it makes sense that community based policing should extend online as well. Moreover, the proper deployment of social media technologies can further strengthen a community's ability to resist crime by creating a digital town hall of sorts for community collaboration on crime prevention strategies. The notion of digital presence is important for the future just as officers check in at various businesses throughout the day the occasional check in on social media has the potential to increase law enforcement visibility in the community and provide access to officers who may be at another location. This increased digital presence should benefit agencies who employ it well by giving the potential criminal and the everyday citizen the sense that police are always present and available.

Given the instantaneous nature and ubiquity of social media applications it is also possible to envision a future in which non-emergency communication between police and the public will rely less on news outlets and phone calls and more on tweets and check-ins (see Bain et al. 2016). For example, one advantage of this instant line of communication is the ability to provide the public with more timely and accurate information about ongoing situations such as road closures. Also as American society's fear of crime continues to rise despite evidence of a 30-year decline in violent crime rates social media provides a future tool for sheriffs and police agencies to highlight their public victories and mitigate community tensions with real-time updates. Given the mainstream media's focus on crime it is often up to local agencies to get the word out when they provide non-crime-related services to the community. Fortunately, social media provides a perfect outlet for disseminating announcements about public service, success stories, and other pertinent information that may not make the evening news cycle or may need immediate widespread distribution.

Nevertheless, the use of social media by law enforcement agencies is still relatively new; in fact, not all agencies make use of social media, nor have access to social media. The 2013 LEMAS study, published in 2015, made a distinction between having a website and actually using social media (see Table 8.2).

Social media is here to stay and will probably have an impact on any agency that actively utilizes its various forms: Facebook, Instagram, Twitter, Pinterest, Vine, Reddit, etc. The greatest limitation of using social media is the restrictive policy of an agency; or not having a policy at all! Otherwise, if incorporated properly, there is no doubt that social media can enhance public trust, communication, and cooperation. Agencies do not have to reinvent the wheel to implement positive social media technologies and

Table 8.2 Local police departments using websites and social media, by size of population served, 2013

Population served	With own website	Using social media
All sizes	60%	58%
1,000,000 or more	100	100
500,000–999,999	100	97
250,000–499,999	98	93
100,000–249,999	97	91
50,000–99,999	97	89
25,000–49,999	93	82
10,000–24,999	90	79
2,500–9,999	67	63
2,499 or fewer	30	36

Source: Reaves, 2015, Law Enforcement Management and Administrative Statistics (LEMAS) Survey, 2013, Table 7

policies; sites like Connected COPS.net (http://connectedcops.net/docu ments-2/policies-and-strategies/) and the IACP Center for Social Media (http://www.iacpsocialmedia.org/) can provide valuable assistance. Both sites have links to articles, policy-related issues, legal concerns, examples of successful utilization by public safety agencies. Guidelines on the "dos and don'ts" can be found at these sites or other online sites for guidance. Of course there are the civil libel concerns as well as controlling whether comments from the public are posted. Agencies must dedicate some personnel to this endeavor if social media use is to be successful – it must be attractive, current, and useful to the public users.

Finally however, it is just as important to note that regardless of our current – personal – understanding, the fact remains that none of this technology is science fiction, but is instead (a) science fact, and with the use of a simple scenario we can illustrate this perfectly.

PUTTING IT ALL TOGETHER – A SCENARIO

Officer Florence Kiaher is being dispatched to a domestic disturbance call in her patrol sector. A subdued tone, emanating from the small stereo speakers mounted on her shoulders and aimed at her ears, lets her know that dispatch information is being sent to her. She speaks the command key to have GPS information for the call displayed on a map in the heads-up display in the vehicle windshield and for the other information to be spoken as well as displayed on the computer screen. The in-car camera system and her body-worn cameras are automatically triggered and a live video feed from all cameras is streamed back to dispatch, available for live viewing if necessary.

Before Officer Kiaher arrives at the location of the call, she learns that a husband, who is apparently intoxicated, is yelling and threatening his wife, that there are two young children living in the residence, that the husband has been arrested for domestic violence in the past, and that another unit is being dispatched to the call. Digital photographs of all occupants of the residence and Automatic License Plate Reader data on the two vehicles registered to the husband and wife have been sent to her on-board computer.

Upon arriving at the scene, the in-car video system has scanned the licensed plates of the car parked in front of the residence and the last car of two parked in the driveway. Officer Kiaher is notified by her computer system that the vehicle in front of the residence is one of the family's vehicles, but the last one in the driveway is owned by another person. The name of that person, along with a photo, is sent to the cruiser computer. As officer Kiaher gets out of her police cruiser, a visor automatically slides down over her eyes and the visor's heads-up display activates. Officer Kiaher looks toward the first vehicle parked in the driveway and one of her body-worn cameras scans the license plate. She is notified that the vehicle is registered to the family.

As she approaches the front door of the residence, a male walks out onto the porch. As Officer Kiaher approaches him, he says that the police are not needed, that the argument was just a typical family feud and all is now calm. The front body-worn camera on Officer Kiaher's uniform scans the subject's face and eyes. In several seconds, the identity of the male is determined to a 95% probability (using facial and iris recognition software and databases). An image of the identified male is sent to Officer Kiaher's in-car computer and transmitted to her visor, where she is able to view the image of the data center's best guess superimposed on the face of the actual subject. She mentally agrees that the computer match is correct. The data center continues to search for any "wants and warrants."

Officer Kiaher's array of body-worn cameras has been observing the movements of the subject that she has been speaking with. A red LED begins flashing in the corner of her visor. The cameras have picked up two indications from the encounter with this subject. First, the subject is displaying body-language consistent with a pending physical attack. Officer Kiaher is warned that she is standing too close to him and should add distance. She moves back several feet. The second indication that was detected by the cameras, from unconscious facial and body movements, is that the subject is probably lying. Officer Kiaher asks the subject to go to the sidewalk and speak to the other officer that will arrive momentarily. She has been notified of the back-up officer's location and knows that he will arrive in approximately 20 seconds. The subject walks off of the porch and toward the street. The body-worn camera array follows his actions and will warn Officer Kiaher if he deviates from his course.

Officer Kiaher enters the residence and speaks to the husband and wife. She goes about the business of handling the call, with her camera and computer systems observing and monitoring. A domestic violence arrest is made, and communications are established with Child Protective Services and with the Victim Assistance Office of the local court. A DNA sample is taken from the husband, who has been arrested, and the sample is transmitted to LDIS (Local DNA Index System); from there it will be sent to CODIS. The sample will be checked against open cases in each system.

With all reports submitted and as a final action, Officer Kiaher now turns to the departments social media page and provides the local community group with information that an arrest was made in a domestic incident, and that all parties are safely accounted for. Although providing no real details of the case, she uses this as an example of the ongoing work being done in the local community to tackle this issue, and provides the contact details of a number of victim awareness and domestic shelters.

Now, consider the consequences of a failure in the technologies, provided for in the situation just described: after Officer Kiaher asks the individual to go wait by the street for the incoming officer, the cameras assessing his movements and implied actions instead relay (incorrectly) that the man is now an imminent threat. Not only is this threat relayed to Officer Kiaher, but it is also relayed to multiple technologies in her patrol car, as well as to dispatch. This presents an array of potential responses, most of which result in harm coming to the individual wrongly assessed. Less-than-lethal deployment might be used against him, dispatch would be alerted to send multiple backup units, or Officer Kiaher, relying on the accuracy of the information relayed to her, may act with lethal force, because the threat level has increased rapidly, and beyond reasonable expectation. Who, then, does the wrongly harmed man turn to for justice?

The use of visors, whilst appropriate for many situations and circumstance, are not always very helpful when confronting a person that may appear already to be agitated or unnerved. Good eye contact is imperative in these types of situations and the visor may create an unwelcome barrier which causes an escalation rather than providing for a sense of calm between the officer and the individual being questioned. Is it wrong to provide information to the community about an arrest taking place? Should we first consider the privacy of the victim in such an intimate case as domestic violence? There is always the possibility that the victim would see this as a private matter and not want those outside of the family unit to have knowledge of the offense. Indeed, Daigle (2013: 121) has stated that with the exception of " … the details we choose to share with others, the give-and-take, the ups and downs, and the good and bad times are largely shared by only us and our partners." Should we be mindful of that fact? Conversely, could providing greater evidence of cases and successful conclusions provide for greater confidence in the system and lead to more victims coming forward? According to Safe Horizon (2016) one in four women in the United States will experience domestic violence in their lifetime. It is something which requires greater discussion. Nevertheless, the benefits of good technology are boundless, with instant data feeds, vehicle and suspect recognition and identification, tracking systems, and officer protection equipment, the state of things to come can only provide for a positive endeavor.

CONCLUSION

Technology, without question, has improved the efficiency and effectiveness of law enforcement at all levels. As Bain states in Chapter 2, this can be evidenced in the introduction of photography, the two-way radio, and crime labs in the first century of modern policing, to the examination of DNA markers and forensic science to examine evidence collected at the crime scene at the end of the second century. There is also little question that technology will continue to improve law enforcement in many ways. Today our technologies provide transparency through the use of recording devices to instant access to critical information in the field, the future of law enforcement technology is exciting and bright. Yet, with financial resources seemingly limited, it will be up to each agency and administrator to decide what is "best technology" for their agency. One area which is utilized correctly has undoubted benefits for both individual officers and their agencies is the inclusion and greater use of social media to help nurture and support greater ties with the community. As was outlined by Bain in Chapter 4 and Robinson in Chapter 5, communication is key, and good communication can provide for a more supportive community, and a more compliant suspect/offender (Barker et al. 2008).

Moving forward, one has only to look at the current state of law enforcement to predict future technologies. The emphasis placed on body cameras and similar devices is only going to increase. These devices are intended to improve officer safety as well as improve community relations and restore trust in police in communities where it has been lost because of the actions of a few (Bain et al. 2014). As a law enforcement practitioner the prospects of these advancements should not only be viewed as exciting, but welcomed. At issue is the ability for law enforcement officers to re-establish what the overwhelming majority of us already know; that police officers are well intended and by and large do the job professionally and within the confines of the Constitution and law. It is the few who have cast a shadow of doubt over the many.

As Conser and Carsone have noted in Chapter 6 (and as we have stated earlier in this chapter) the issue of safety is also likely to play a dominant role in future technologies. There are numerous examples in the past several years of police officers being executed while on duty. In December of 2015, a police officer from Danville, Ohio, was found shot dead in his municipal building's parking lot after a caller to the police dispatch center warned that her boyfriend left her residence with weapons and wanted to kill a police officer. The officer never answered the radio call to warn him about the threat.

Will technology be developed that will allow a police officer to have better situational awareness and more knowledge about what is going on around them, even when they can't see what's around them? Will information technologies used on the battlefield be modified to be used by police officers – such as the move to using drones? It is hard to know what the future holds, but the interest in using technology to make officers safer is never likely to wane.

For all the technological advancements that have already benefited law enforcement, it is still hard to imagine exactly what the law enforcement landscape will look like in 30 (plus) years. Thirty years ago few could have imagined the technology that we use today.

REFERENCES

Accenture. (2013). *Preparing police services for the future: Six steps toward transformation.* Dublin, Ireland: Accenture Global Services Limited. Available at: https://www.accenture.com/us-en/insight-preparing-police-service-future-six-steps-toward-transformation.aspx.

Advertisement. (2015, March/April). Greater utility. *Law Enforcement Product News, 26*(3), 4.

APCO. (2007, August). A watching brief with body worn devices. *Bapco Journal, 13*(8), 6–7. Available at: http://www.bapco.org.uk/content/media/7758/bapco_aug_2007_.pdf.

Bain, A., Brooks, G., Golding, B., Ellis, T., & Lewis, C. (2016). Calling the police: The use of non-emergency 101in England and Wales. *Police Journal: Theory, Practice & Principles, 89*, 1–15.

Bain, A., Robinson, B. K., & Conser, J. (2014). Perceptions of policing: Improving communication in local communities. *International Journal of Police, Science & Management, 16*(4), 267–276.

Barker, V., Giles, H., Hajek, C., Ota, H., Noels, K., Lim, T.-S., & Somera, L. (2008). Police communication. Why does it matter? *Communication Currents, 3*(3). Available at: https://www.natcom.org/CommCurrentsArticle.aspx?id=886.

Bignami, F. (2015). The US legal system on data protection in the field of law enforcement. Safeguards, Rights and Remedies for EU Citizens. LIBE Committee: GWU Law School Public Law Research Paper No. 2015-54. Available at: SSRN: http://ssrn.com/abstract=2705618.

Carsone, L. P., & Conser, J. A. (1984, February). Silicon streets blue. *Law and Order Magazine*, *54*, 18–21.

Conser, J. A., & Frissora, G. G. (2007). The patrol function in the future – One vision. In J. Schafer, (Ed.), *Policing 2020: Exploring the future of crime, communities, and policing* Quantico VA: Futures Working Group.

Daigle, L. E. (2013). *Victimology: The essentials.* London: Sage Publications.

Farb, R. L. (2002). The fourth amendment, privacy, and law enforcement. *Popular Government*, (Spring): 13–19.

Galvin, B. (2015, March). Predictive policing software. *Law Officer Magazine*, *11*(3), 20–23.

Gitlin, J. M. (2015, July 2. Heads-up displays in cars can hinder driver safety. Cars Technica: All Things Automotive. Available at: http://arstechnica.com/cars/2015/07/heads-up-displays-in-cars-can-hinder-driver-safety/.

Glennon, J. (2008, March 12). Pre-attack indicators: Conscious recognition of telegraphed cues. *PoliceOne.com*. Available at: http://www.policeone.com/police-products/training/articles/1660205-Pre-attack-indicators-Conscious-recognition-of-telegraphed-cues/.

Hernandez, D. (2015, June 4). The new Google photos app is disturbingly good at data-mining your photos. *Fusion*. Available at: http://fusion.net/story/142326/the-new-google-photos-app-is-disturbingly-good-at-data-mining-your-photos/.

Hollywood, J. S., Woods, D., Silberglitt, R., & Jackson, B. A. (2015). *Using future Internet technologies to strengthen criminal justice.* Washington, DC: National Institute of Justice and the RAND Corporation.

Horizon, S. (2016). Domestic violence: Statistics & facts, *Safehorizon*. *Moving Victims of Violence from Crisis to Confidence*. Available at: http://www.safehorizon.org/page/domestic-violence-statistics–facts-52.html.

Kennedy, T. J. (2015, May). Get to know FirstNet. *Law Enforcement Technology*, *42*(5), 23–25.

Krahnstoever, N. (2011, August). *Automated detection and prevention of disorderly and criminal activities.* (Document No. 235579) [Unpublished]. Available at: https://www.ncjrs.gov/pdffiles1/nij/grants/235579.pdf.

Kraska, P. B. (2007). Militarization and policing – Its relevance to 21st century police. *Policing: A Journal of Policy and Practice*, *1*(4), 501–513.

Kraska, P. B., & Kappeler, V. E. (1997). Militarizing American Police: The rise and normalization of paramilitary units. *Social Problems*, *44*(1), 1–18.

Krebs, B. (2015). *Spam Nation*. Naperville, IL: Sourcebooks.

Lytle, D. J., & Randa, R. (2015). The effects of police satisfaction on fear of crime in a semi-rural setting. *International Criminal Justice Review*, *25*(4), 301–317.

Madhani, A. (2015, August 6). Motorola: High-tech future for police includes smartbelts and drones, *USA Today*. Available at: http://www.usatoday.com/story/tech/2015/08/06/motorola-high-tech-future-police-includes-smartbelts-and-drones/31211027/.

McCullough, D. R. C., & Spence, D. L. (2012). American policing in 2022, (Eds.) U.S. Department of Justice, COPS Office. Available at: http://ric-zai-inc.com/Publications/cops-p235-pub.pdf.

Melekain, B. K., & Wexler, M. (2013, May). *Social media and tactical considerations for law enforcement.* Washington, DC: COPS and Police Executive Research Forum. Available at: http://www.policeforum.org/assets/docs/Free_Online_Documents/Technology/social%20media%20and%20tactical%20considerations%20for%20law%20enforcement%202013.pdf.

Newcombe, T. (2014, September 26). Forecasting the future for technology and policing. Available at: http://www.govtech.com/public-safety/Forecasting-the-Future-for-Technology-and-Policing.html.

Pepitone, J. (2013). *What your wireless carrier knows about you.* Available at: http://money.cnn.com/2013/12/16/technology/mobile/wireless-carrier-sell-data/.

PlateSmart. (n.d.). PlateSmart benefits – More than just real-time data. Available at: http://www.platesmart.com/public-safety-commentary/#c.

Police Executive Research Forum. (2014). *Future trends in policing.* Washington, DC: Office of Community Oriented Policing Services. Available at: http://www.policeforum.org/assets/docs/Free_Online_Documents/Leadership/future%20trends%20in%20policing%202014.pdf.

Risley, D. (2015, July). Private police coming to a neighborhood near you! why private police may be an important element of future law enforcement. *The Police Chief, 82.* Available at: http://www.policechiefmagazine.org/magazine/index.cfm?fuseaction=display&article_id=3770&issue_id=72015.

Sancier, G. (2012, September 17). How 'profiling' can save your life. *PoliceOne. com.* Available at: http://www.policeone.com/Officer-Safety/articles/5981617-How-profiling-can-save-your-life/.

Schafer, J. (Ed.). (2007). *Policing 2020: Exploring the future of crime, communities, and policing.* Quantico VA: Futures Working Group.

Scherer, J. R., & Jarvis, J. P. (2011). *The future of law enforcement: A consideration of potential allies and adversaries,* (Vol. 7). Proceedings of the Futures Working Group. Quantico, VA: Futures Working Group.

Sen, R., & Borle, S. (2015). Estimating the contextual risk of data breach: An empirical approach. *Journal of Management Information Systems, 32*(2), 314–341.

Silberglitt, R., Chow, B. G., Hollywood, J. H., Woods, D., Zaydman, M., & Jackson, B. A. (2015). *Visions of law enforcement technology in the period 2024–2034.* Santa Monica, CA: RAND Corporation. Available at: http://www.rand.org/content/dam/rand/pubs/research_reports/RR900/RR908/RAND_RR908.pdf.

Treverton, G. F., Wollman, M., Wilke, E., & Lai, D. (2011). *Moving toward the future of policing.* Santa Monica, CA: RAND Corporation.

Verhoeven, P. (Director), & Schmiidt, A. (Producer). (1987). *Robocop [motion picture]*. USA: Orion Pictures.
Wakefield, J. (2013, July 3). Future cops: How technology is set to change policing. *BBC News*. Available at: http://www.bbc.com/news/technology-22954783

Andy Bain is Assistant Professor of Criminal Justice at the University of Mount Union, Ohio, USA. He holds a PhD in Offender Behavior, a MSc in Criminal Justice, and a Graduate Diploma in Psychology. Andy is the coauthor of *Outlaw Motorcycle Gangs: A Theoretical Perspective* (with Mark Lauchs & Peter Bell), and previously coauthored *Professional Risk Taking with People: A Guide to Decision-Making in Health, Social Care & Criminal Justice* (with David Carson). In addition Andy has published in a number of leading international academic and professional journals. His professional background includes 4 years with the National Probation Service (England & Wales) and 6 years running a successful criminal justice consultancy group, providing guidance and advice to offender groups, law enforcement agencies and correctional bodies. This, in turn led to the publication of a number of local and national policing and corrections reports. He is an active member of national and international professional bodies, and his research interests include tattoo and culture, gangs and coded language; policing and social groups; social-psychology of offending and risk-taking behavior; and the (psychological) investigation of criminal behavior.

Louis P. Carsone is the Director of Public Safety for the City of Hubbard, Ohio, USA. He is a retired Police Officer of the City after 31 years of full-time service, having served as a Patrol Sergeant and Police Chief. He holds a bachelor's degree in Law Enforcement Administration and a Master of Science degree in Criminal Justice, both from the Youngstown State University. He has authored several articles on the topic of law enforcement use of computers and has instructed courses on police use of computer technology. He is currently certified as a Basic Police Academy Instructor in Ohio, instructing for several local Police Academies.

James A. Conser is Professor Emeritus at Youngstown State University (Ohio), Adjunct Professor at the University of Mount Union and currently the Criminal Justice Internship Coordinator in the Sociology and Criminal Justice Department. He previously served as the Deputy Director of the Ohio Peace Officer Training Commission (OPOTC) from January of 1999 through December of 2002. Jim holds a PhD in Higher Education Administration and a MSc in Criminal Justice. Jim began his career as a police officer in Arlington County, Virginia. He is a Certified Protection Professional through ASIS International. He is coauthor of *Law Enforcement in the United States* (2013) and *Police Personnel Systems* (1983). He is a lifetime member of the Society of Police Futurists International (PFI) and was national secretary for 9 years. He is also a lifetime member of the Academy of Criminal Justice Sciences, a member of the Ohio Crime Prevention Association, and the Ohio Criminal Justice Education Association.

Brandon J. Courtney teaches as a Developmental English Tutor at Passaic County Community College in Paterson, New Jersey, and is an Adjunct Instructor at Hollins University's Tinker Mountain Writers' Workshop Online. An accomplished poet, Brandon has two full-length collections, *The Grief Muscles* (Sheep Meadow Press) and *Rooms for Rent in the Burning City* (Spark Wheel Press). Additionally, he has a chapbook and full-length collection forthcoming from YesYes Books in 2016 and 2017, respectively. Brandon is a veteran of the United States Navy, and received his BA from Drake University in English Writing. He also received his MFA in Creative Writing from Hollins University in 2012, and attended the University of Chicago's MLA program.

William J. Mackey is an Assistant Professor in the Department of Criminology and Criminal Justice at Indiana State University. His research interests include: Cyber-criminology, Social Engineering, Technological Advances in Corrections and Crime Prevention, White-Collar Crime, and Criminological Theory. Bill's current research is focused on correlates of human behavior in data breaches and the application of criminological theory to cybercrime and breach prevention. Bill has published work in the areas of social engineering, advanced crime prevention technologies, and individual differences in both white-collar offenders and hackers. Mr. Mackey is a member of the Cincinnati Bell Digital Forensics Working Group, the National White-Collar Crime Research Consortium, Infragard Partnership for Protection, and the American Society of Criminology. He received a dual bachelor's degree in Psychology and Criminology from Iowa State University, a Master's degree in Criminology from Indiana State University, and is in the process of completing requirements for his PhD in Criminology at the University of Cincinnati.

Bryan K. Robinson is a criminologist with research interest in lethal violence, criminological theory and media depictions of crime. Bryan completed his Doctoral degree in Sociology at the State University of New York, Albany in 2012. His dissertation examined the role of religious institutions on suicide and homicide rates in U.S. counties. His current research includes an analysis of census data and state corrections data to assess the effect of religious, family, and economic variables on county level recidivism rates. Bryan has published on Team-Based Learning Methods, media depictions of family life, and international research on teen suicide rates. He currently teaches a range of classes on the undergraduate program at the University of Mount Union (Ohio), which includes: Introduction to Sociology, Introduction to Criminology, Sociology of Violence, Media and Society, and Drugs and Society.

Andrew Turowski is the Chief of Police for the City of Louisville (Ohio). He has 24 years of police experience with assignments to patrol, investigations, the Stark County Metropolitan narcotics unit, a FBI Violent Crimes Fugitive Task Force, and a FBI Joint Terrorism Task Force. He also served in the U.S. Army Military Police Corps. He is a member of the Ohio Association of Chiefs of Police where he is a Certified Law Enforcement Executive (CLEE). He has a Master's Degree in Public Administration and serves as an adjunct professor at Kent State University and the University of Mount Union.

INDEX

© The Author(s) 2016
A. Bain (ed.), *Law Enforcement and Technology*,
DOI 10.1057/978-1-137-57915-7